teach® yourself

quick fix
spanish grammar

D1331672

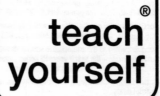

quick fix
spanish grammar
keith chambers

For over 60 years, more than
40 million people have learnt over
750 subjects the **teach yourself**
way, with impressive results.

be where you want to be
with **teach yourself**

For UK order enquiries: please contact Bookpoint Ltd, 130 Milton Park, Abingdon, Oxon OX14 4SB. Telephone: +44 (0)1235 827720. Fax: +44 (0)1235 400454. Lines are open 09.00–18.00, Monday to Saturday, with a 24-hour message answering service. Details about our titles and how to order are available at www.teachyourself.co.uk

For USA order queries: please contact McGraw-Hill Customer Services, P.O. Box 545, Blacklick, OH 43004-0545, USA. Telephone: 1-800-722-4726. Fax: 1-614-755-5645.

For Canada order queries: please contact McGraw-Hill Ryerson Ltd, 300 Water St, Whitby, Ontario L1N 9B6, Canada. Telephone: 905 430 5000. Fax: 905 430 5020.

Long renowned as the authoritative source for self-guided learning – with more than 40 million copies sold worldwide – the **teach yourself** series includes over 300 titles in the fields of languages, crafts, hobbies, business, computing and education.

British Library Cataloguing in Publication Data: a catalogue entry for this title is available from The British Library.

Library of Congress Catalog Card Number: on file

First published in UK 2003 by Hodder Education, 338 Euston Road, London, NW1 3BH.

First published in US 2003 by Contemporary Books, a Division of the McGraw-Hill Companies, 1 Prudential Plaza, 130 East Randolph Street, Chicago, IL 60601 USA.

The **teach yourself** name is a registered trade mark of Hodder Headline.

Typeset by Transet Limited, Coventry, England.
Printed in Great Britain for Hodder Education, a division of Hodder Headline, 338 Euston Road, London NW1 3BH by Cox & Wyman Ltd, Reading, Berkshire.

Hodder Headline's policy is to use papers that are natural, renewable and recyclable products and made from wood grown in sustainable forests. The logging and manufacturing processes are expected to conform to the environmental regulations of the country of origin.

Impression number	10 9 8 7 6 5 4
Year	2007 2006 2005

contents

This basic grammar is designed as a handy reference for someone who has recently started Spanish or who would like to revise some of the important points of the language in a systematic way.

The book is divided into units, each summarizing a specific grammatical point, with related exercises. Answers are provided at the end of the book.

Most learners find that regular, but limited, targeted practice is the most helpful way to get on in a language and make real progress. Use the contents page to identify a point you particularly want to revise and set yourself a specific goal to practise as time allows. You need not work through the book in rigid order.

Explanations have deliberately been kept as simple as possible and err on the side of general correctness for the beginner; however, to provide an insight into how the language works. I have also included some examples of more advanced use.

My thanks go to my students past and present who have experienced and helped to refine the contents of this basic grammar. I hope you too will find it useful and informative.

Keith Chambers

Spanish spelling is very straightforward. The rules are logical and universally applied.

A The Spanish alphabet contains the following letters; their names (i.e. the way they are pronounced individually) are given in brackets.

A (a)   B (be)   C (ce)   CH (che)   D (de)   E (e)   F (efe)
G (ge)   H (ache)   I (i)   J (jota)   K (ka)   L (ele)   LL (elle)
M (eme)   N (ene)   Ñ (eñe)   O (o)   P (pe)   Q (cu)
R (ere)   S (ese)   T (te)   U (u)   V (uve)   W (uve doble)
X (equis)   Y (i griega)   Z (zeta)

K and w are rarely used and are found in words borrowed from other languages: kilo, whisky, etc. In older dictionaries, the letters **ch**, **ll** and **ñ** follow c, l and n as separate entries. Few words actually start with **ñ**.

B The good news is that Spanish spelling follows how the word is pronounced:

suéter *sweater*; fútbol *football*; foto *photo*; champú *shampoo*

Notice how Spanish spells words which seem so familiar to us:

posible; profesor; necesario; expresión; pasión; nacional; cuestión; inmenso

C Spanish avoids double consonants except with four exceptions, which you can remember by applying the CaRoLiNe rule.

- **cc**: diccionario *dictionary*, acción *action*, acceso *access*, where the **c** has two different sounds;
- **rr**: terrible, horror, Inglaterra *England*, where the **r** sound has double strength;
- **ll**: millón *million*, guerrilla, llama *flame*, where the **ll** is a different sound from **l**;
- **nn** (much less common): innecesario *unnecessary*, innegable *undeniable*, where an existing word starting with **n** has added a prefix.

D Z is not permitted before **e** or **i**; **c** is used instead: cebra *zebra*; cero *zero*

E Where you want to write a **kw** sound, use **cu**: cuestión.

Where you want to write a **k** sound in front of **e** or **i**, use **qu**: quiosco, tranquilo, querer *to want*; otherwise use **c**: catorce *fourteen*.

To write a **g** sound (as in *go*), use **gu** in front of **e** or **i**: guerra *war*, Miguel *Michael*, espaguetis *spaghetti*; otherwise use **g** as in English: gol *goal*.

A **g** on its own in front of **e** or **i** sounds like a Spanish **j** (i.e. a strongly aspirated **h**): general, Gibraltar, genuino, gitano *gypsy*.

A very few words have a **gw** sound in front of **e** or **i**: in this case, the spelling is **gü**: cigüeña *stork*. In front of **a** or **o**; use **gu** with no dots: guante *glove*.

Spanish needs to spell some words with an accent. Fortunately, the rules are fairly simple and logical.

The accent mark (´), always placed over the stressed vowel, is used in four main circumstances.

A To distinguish two words of different meaning: **si** *if*, **sí** *yes*; **mi** *my*, **mí** (*me* after a preposition); **tu** *your*, **tú** *you*; **como** *like*, **cómo** *how*.

B To distinguish a question word from a relative pronoun: **dónde** *where?*, **qué** *what?*, **cuándo** *when?*, **por qué** *why?*, **quién** *who?*.

NB **Cómo** *how* always has an accent.

C To distinguish pronouns from similarly spelt adjectives: **este libro** *this book*, **éste es mi libro** *this (one) is my book*.

D To indicate some irregularity in stress (probably the most important use).

• Spanish words are normally stressed on the final syllable, unless the word ends in a vowel, **s** or **n**, where the stress falls on the last-but-one syllable.

usted, Madrid, azul, Gibraltar

BUT

casa, Inglaterra, cinco, comen, casas

• Any exception is indicated with an accent: habitación, fútbol, física, veintidós, inglés.

- Bearing this in mind, note what happens when endings are added to certain types of words.

inglés *English (m.)* → inglesa *English (f.)*;
habitación *room* → habitaciones *rooms*;
volumen *volume* → volúmenes *volumes*.

- Sometimes other changes occur to fit in with the spelling rules.

lápiz *pencil* → lápices *pencils*
actriz *actress* → actrices *actresses*
un libro *one book* → veintiún libros *21 books*

You'll soon get the hang of it if you practise saying new words out loud. Say the word first, then write down what you hear!

exercise

The following words sound very much like English but have an accent mark missing. Say each word out loud and write the accent mark on the correct vowel.

a lamina	**c** Peru	**e** limite	**g** futbol
b Dali	**d** Bogota	**f** cafe	**h** medico

Make the necessary spelling or accent changes to the second word in each pair.

i feroz/ferozes	**l** sigo/siges
j francesa/frances	**m** hice/hico
k posiciones/posicion	**n** Paco/Pacita

Nouns in Spanish are either masculine or feminine. The gender is frequently obvious from the spelling.

A Most nouns which end in **-o** are masculine. The word for *the (the definite article)* with a masculine noun in the singular is **el**: el libro *the book*; el colegio *the (high) school*; el niño *the child*; el chico *the boy, lad*; el vino *the wine*; el periódico *the newspaper*.

B Nouns which denote males are usually masculine: el hombre *the man*; el padre *the father*; el estudiante *the student*; el profesor *the teacher*; el director *the director*; el cantante *the singer*; el ladrón *the robber*; el señor *the gentleman*.

C Nouns ending in **-a** are usually feminine. The definite article with a feminine singular noun is **la**: la casa *the house*; la cerveza *the beer*; la revista *the magazine*; la chica *the girl*; la niña *the child*; la señora *the lady*.

D Nouns which denote females are usually feminine: la mujer *the woman*; la madre *the mother*; la cantante *the singer*; la directora *the director*.

E Nouns which end in **-e** may be masculine or feminine, so you will need to learn the gender.

- Common masculine nouns ending in -e include: el café *the coffee, café*; el cine *the cinema*; el aceite *the oil*; el té *the tea*; el jefe *the chief, boss*.

- Nouns ending in **-aje** are masculine: el garaje *the garage*; el peaje *toll* (*on motorway*, etc.); el equipaje *luggage, equipment*.

- Common feminine nouns ending in **-e** include: la clase *the class*; la llave *the key*; la gente *the people*; la torre *the tower*.

exercise

Put the correct definite article (*el/la*) with these nouns.

E.g. libro → el libro

a vino

b cerveza

c casa

d colegio

e chico

f chica

g periódico

h revista

i niña

j niño

Now put the correct definite article (*el/la*) with the following nouns.

k clase

l llave

m aceite

n gente

o cine

p garaje

q madre

r té

s café

t equipaje

u torre

This unit looks at nouns whose gender is not so obvious.

A Nouns which end in a consonant can belong to either gender, so you will need to learn these carefully.

• Some masculine nouns ending in a consonant include: el papel *the paper*; el cartel *the poster*; el arroz *the rice*; el lápiz *the pencil*; el andaluz *the Andalusian*.

• Some feminine words ending in a consonant include: la luz *the light*; la piel *the skin*; la habitación *the room*; la capital *the capital city*; la catedral *the cathedral*.

• All nouns ending in **-dad** or **-tad** are feminine: la ciudad *the city, large town*; la universidad *the university*; la libertad *the liberty*; la verdad *the truth*.

B The word for *a / an* (the indefinite article) is **un** for masculine nouns and **una** for feminine nouns: un libro *a book* un cine *a cinema*; un lápiz *a pencil*; una casa *a house*; una universidad *a university*; una habitación *a room*.

C To make all nouns plural, add **-s** to words ending in a vowel and **-es** to words ending in a consonant. The word for *the* is **los** with masculine plural nouns and **las** with feminine plural nouns: los chicos *the boys*; los profesores *the teachers*; las chicas *the girls*; las universidades *the universities*.

• Nouns ending in **-z** change to **-ces** in the plural: los lápices *the pencils*; los andaluces *the Andalusians*.

- Nouns ending in **-ión**, like **habitación** *room*, lose the accent when adding **-es**: las habitaciones *the rooms*.

- Some plurals which are masculine can include the feminine: los hijos *the sons and daughters, children*; los padres *the parents*; los tíos *the aunts and uncles*.

NB If there is likely to be any ambiguity, you can clarify what you mean by re-stating the nouns: los tíos y las tías *the uncles and the aunts*.

exercise

Give the correct definite aticle (*el/la*) with these nouns.

E.g. catedral → la catedral

a luz	**f** papel
b arroz	**g** andaluz
c ciudad	**h** habitación
d piel	**i** lápiz
e cartel	**j** catedral

Give the correct indefinite article (*un/una*) with the same nouns.

E.g. una catedral

Change the same nouns into the plural, adding *los* or *las* as appropriate.

E.g. las catedrales

This unit looks at nouns that are feminine by exception.

You already know some basic rules for genders of nouns. There are, however, some nouns which, from their endings, appear to be of one gender when in fact they are of the other.

A There are a very few nouns which end in **-o**, but which are, in fact, feminine. These are mostly words which have been shortened: la radio(grafía) *radio*; la foto(grafía) *photograph*; la moto(cicleta) *motorbike*; la disco(teca) *disco*. These nouns take feminine articles.

NB el radio *radius* or *radium*; American Spanish sometimes uses **el radio** for *a radio set* instead of **la radio**.

The following masculine-looking nouns are also feminine: la modelo *(female) fashion model*; la mano *hand* (because it was feminine in Latin!).

Esta chica es una modelo muy hermosa.	*This girl is a very beautiful model.*
Dame la mano.	*Give me your hand.*

B Adjectives will also agree in the feminine.

Tengo una buena foto de Julio.	*I've got a good photograph of Julio.*
Su moto nueva es fantástica.	*His new motorbike is great.*
un coche de segunda mano	*a second-hand car*

NB a la (mano) derecha/izquierda *on the right / left.*

A la (mano) derecha está
  la catedral.

*On the right (-hand
  side) is the cathedral.*

exercise

Crucigrama. All the answers are feminine words ending in -o.

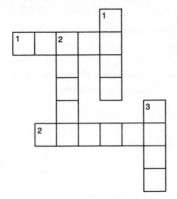

HORIZONTALES
1 ¿Hay un programa en la …?
2 Juanita es una … fantástica.

VERTICALES
1 Tengo una … de Julio.
2 Vamos a la …
3 Vamos en tu …

Many nouns which end in -*a* and which look feminine are masculine. This unit summarizes these.

A An important group is formed of 'international' words of Greek origin, which end in **-ma**. Their meaning in English is generally obvious: el dilema *dilemma*; el problema *problem*; el sistema *system*; el esquema *scheme*; el drama *drama*; el programa *program(me)*; el telegrama *telegram*; el tema *theme*.

B Other miscellaneous masculine words ending in -a include: el cometa *comet*; el tranvía *tram*; el mapa *map* and nouns denoting a male person, such as: el atleta *athlete*; el guía *guide*; el policía *policeman*; el trompeta *trumpet player*; el corneta *bugler*; el batería *drummer*.

You will come across some of these nouns with feminine articles, which gives them a different meaning: la cometa *kite*; la trompeta *trumpet*; la corneta *bugle*; la batería *drum kit*.

C Nouns ending in **-ista** are masculine unless specifically referring to a female: el periodista *journalist*; el turista *tourist*; el dentista *dentist*; el futbolista *footballer* and political words such as **socialista**.

D Some words can be either masculine or feminine, but with a different meaning: la consonante *consonant*, el consonante *word rhyming with another*; la orden *order, command*, el orden *arrangement, tidiness*; la disco *discoteque*, el disco *record, disc*; la capital *capital (city)*, el capital *capital (money)*;

la manzanilla *camomile tea*, el manzanilla *type of fortified wine*; la cólera *anger, rage*, el cólera *cholera*.

NB A few nouns in recent years have evolved forms (not always officially recognized) to denote females, such as: la jefa *boss* (from el **jefe**); la presidenta *president* (from el **presidente**); la estudianta *student* (from el **estudiante**).

exercise

Put the most appropriate article (*el, la, un, una*) with these nouns.

E.g. Quiero comprar _____ moto diferente. → Quiero comprar una moto diferente.

a ¿Tienes _____ foto de Luisa?
b Hay _____ programa en _____ radio.
c Tengo _____ moto verde.
d Vamos a _____ disco. Quiero bailar _____ chachachá.
e Quiero ver el museo. ¿Es usted _____ guía, señor?
f Juan López es _____ atleta internacional.
g No puedo ver _____ mapa – no tengo mis gafas.
h Julia es _____ modelo en _____ foto.
i Julio tiene _____ mano en escayola (*in plaster*).
j Vamos en _____ tranvía número uno.

This unit groups more nouns according to gender.

A Nouns which end in **-aje**, like **el garaje** *the garage*, are masculine (see Unit 3). Also masculine are most nouns ending in a stressed syllable: el valor *valour*; el amor *love*; el honor *honour*; el champú *shampoo*; el rubí *ruby*; el bailarín *dancer*.

- The days of the week and months of the year (see Unit 12) are masculine: el lunes *Monday*; el septiembre pasado *last September*.

- Countries are masculine unless ending in unstressed **-a**: Perú *Peru*; Canadá *Canada*; los Estados Unidos *the USA*; Portugal *Portugal*.

  But España *Spain*; Francia *France*; Inglaterra *England* and many more are feminine as the final **-a** is not stressed.

B Compound nouns are masculine: el lavaplatos *dishwasher*; el paraguas *umbrella*; el limpiacristales *window cleaner*; el cumpleaños *birthday*.

To make compound nouns plural, simply change **el** to **los**: los paraguas *the umbrellas*.

C Unit 4 told you that nouns ending in **-dad** or **-tad** are feminine: la ciudad *city*; la facultad *faculty*. Nouns in **-tud** are likewise feminine: la multitud *crowd*.

- Also feminine are nouns which end in **-umbre**: la cumbre *summit*; la muchedumbre *crowd*.

- Nouns ending in -is and -ie are usually feminine: la crisis *crisis*; la serie *series*.

- Nouns of more than one syllable ending in -ión are usually feminine: la habitación *room*; la reunión *meeting*.

D Nouns beginning with a stressed **a-** or **ha-** but which are feminine take **el** (not **la**) as their singular definite article and **un** as their singular indefinite article: el agua *water*, las aguas *the waters*; el hambre *hunger*; un harpa *a harp*; un hacha *an axe, hatchet*; el águila *eagle*.

exercise

Put in the correct definite article.

E.g. ciudad → la ciudad

a valor	**f** muchedumbre
b champú	**g** multitud
c lunes	**h** crisis
d rubí	**i** reunión
e amor	**j** serie

Which countries are the odd ones out in gender?

k Portugal, Cuba, Perú

l Australia, Canadá, Uruguay

m Japón, Pakistán, China

n Chile, España, Panamá

This unit explains when you need to put in *el*, *la*, *los* or *las* in Spanish.

A In Units 3 and 4 we saw the definite articles according to gender (masculine or feminine) and number (singular or plural).

	masculine	feminine
singular	el libro *the book*	la casa *the house*
plural	los libros *the books*	las casas *the houses*

Generally speaking, the inclusion or omission of the definite article is similar in English and Spanish.

Los tomates son buenos.	*The tomatoes are good.*
¿Tiene usted el número?	*Do you have the number?*
¿Tiene usted el pan y la fruta?	*Do you have the bread and the fruit?*
¿Tiene usted pan y fruta?	*Do you have bread and fruit?*
Hablo inglés.	*I speak English.*
¿Hay pan?	*Is there (any) bread?*

B Spanish, however, includes the article if making a general statement.

Los tomates son horribles.	*(All) tomatoes are horrible.*
No me gusta el vino.	*I don't like (any) wine.*
El inglés es difícil.	*English is difficult.*

C Spanish also includes the article with locations such as school, work, university, town, unlike English.

Estudia en la universidad.	*He's studying at university.*
Emilia está en la iglesia.	*Emilia is in church.*
Voy al trabajo.	*I'm going to work.*
Hay un programa bueno en la televisión.	*There's a good programme on TV.*

D The article is used with titles when talking about someone.

¿Dónde está el señor López?	*Where is Mr López?*
La señorita García no está aquí.	*Miss García is not here.*

But: **Buenos días, señor López.** *Good morning, Mr López.*

Spanish uses the definite article with countries only if the country is limited in some way. Note, however, la India *India*, el Japón *Japan*.

España es bonita.	*Spain is pretty.*
Vivía en la España de Franco.	*He lived in Franco's Spain.*

exercise

Translate the following into English.

a El español es bonito.

b Teresa no habla español.

c Vivimos en la India.

d No me gusta el señor Gómez.

e Buenos días, señora García.

The indefinite article (*a*, *an*) in Spanish agrees in gender (masculine or feminine) with its noun. This unit summarizes the main uses of the indefinite article.

	masculine	feminine
definite	el hombre *the man*	la casa *the house*
indefinite	un hombre *a man*	una casa *a house*

A **Una** changes to **un** in front of a feminine noun or adjective beginning with a stressed **a-** or **ha-**, but not if the **a-** or **ha-** is unstressed.

un arpa *a harp*; un hacha *an axe*; un alta montaña *a high mountain*; una ardilla *a squirrel*; una habitación *a room*

B Spanish also has plural forms of the indefinite article, **unos** (masculine) and **unas** (feminine): unos tirantes *(a pair of) braces*.

The plural forms **unos** and **unas** can also mean *some*.

Hay unos hombres en la esquina.	*There are some men on the corner.*
Creo que hay unas galletas en la cocina.	*I think there are some biscuits in the kitchen.*

C The use of the indefinite article is generally similar to English.

Una chica canta en un coro.	*A girl is singing in a choir.*
Un niño juega con un perro.	*A boy plays with a dog.*

There are some differences, however.

- The indefinite article is not used after **ser** *to be* or **hacerse** *to become* to denote professions, status, etc.

  Soy estudiante.   *I'm a student.*
  Mi padre es mecánico.   *My father is a mechanic.*
  Juan se hizo cantante.   *Juan became a singer.*

- It is not generally used after **tener** *to have* in the negative.

  No tengo familia.   *I haven't got a family.*

- The indefinite article is usually omitted with **sin** *without* and **con** *with*.

  Lo abrí sin llave.   *I opened it without a key.*

- It is not used with **otro** *other*, **cierto** *certain*, or **tal** *such a …*

  Quiero otra habitación.   *I want another room.*

exercise

Put the indefinite article instead of *el* or *la* with the noun.

E.g. la botella (*bottle*) → una botella

a la naranja (*orange*)   **e** la mesa (*table*)
b el plátano (*banana*)   **f** el coche (*car*)
c la manzana (*apple*)   **g** la luz (*light*)
d el chico (*boy*)   **h** la ciudad (*city, town*)

Put *un* or *una* with the following nouns.

i habitación (*room*)   **l** autora (*author*)
j hospital (m.) (*hospital*)   **m** actriz (*actress*)
k aldea (*village*)   **n** ala (*wing*)

Spanish uses cardinal numbers when counting. Here we explain how the numbers from zero to 99 work.

0 cero	15 quince	30 treinta
1 uno/una	16 dieciséis	31 treinta y
2 dos	17 diecisiete	uno/una/un
3 tres	18 dieciocho	32 treinta y dos
4 cuatro	19 diecinueve	33 treinta y tres
5 cinco	20 veinte	40 cuarenta
6 seis	21 veintiuno/veintiuna	41 cuarenta y
7 siete	22 veintidós	uno/una/un
8 ocho	23 veintitrés	42 cuarenta y dos
9 nueve	24 veinticuatro	50 cincuenta
10 diez	25 veinticinco	60 sesenta
11 once	26 veintiséis	70 setenta
12 doce	27 veintisiete	80 ochenta
13 trece	28 veintiocho	90 noventa
14 catorce	29 veintinueve	99 noventa y nueve

A **Uno** becomes **una** in front of a feminine noun; **veintiuno** becomes **veintiuna**.

una casa *one house*; veintiuna casas *21 houses*

B **Uno** becomes **un** in front of any masculine noun; **veintiuno** becomes **veintiún**. These changes also occur in front of a feminine noun beginning with a stressed **a-** or **ha-**.

un libro *one book*; veintiún libros *21 books*; veintiún hachas *21 axes*

NB Take special care when spelling **cuatro**, **catorce** and **quince**!

C All tens and units are linked with **y**. The numbers 16 to 19 and 21 to 29 may also be written as three separate words in older spelling: diez y seis; veinte y uno; veinte y dos, etc.

D 100 is **cien**. **Cien** becomes **ciento** in front of another lesser number.

Tengo cien dólares.	*I have 100 dollars.*
ciento noventa y nueve	*199*

E To say the numbers between 100 and 199, you simply join up the numbers with **ciento**.

Me faltan ciento cincuenta y una libras.	*I'm 151 pounds short.*

Remember to make **uno** agree with a feminine noun.

exercise

Write or say the following in full.

E.g. 23 días → veintitrés días

a 16 años	**d** 9 meses	**g** 21 hombres
b 1 euro	**e** 10 chicas	**h** 1 águila
c 4 casas	**f** 28 días	**i** 2 cervezas

11 numbers above 200

This unit looks at numbers from 200. The hundreds have masculine and feminine forms.

200 doscientos/doscientas	600 seiscientos/seiscientas
300 trescientos/trescientas	700 setecientos/setecientas
400 cuatrocientos/cuatrocientas	800 ochocientos/ochocientas
500 quinientos/quinientas	900 novecientos/novecientas

A Note the agreements in the following:

doscientas treinta y una casas	*231 houses*
cuatrocientos un euros	*401 euro*
quinientas cincuenta y una libras	*551 pounds*
seiscientos sesenta y un hombres	*661 men*

B Numbers above 999:

1.000	mil
2.000	dos mil
3.000	tres mil, etc.
100.000	cien mil
999.000	novecientos noventa y nueve mil
1.000.000	un millón
2.000.000	dos millones, etc.

The same rules of agreement as above apply.

Novecientas noventa y nueve mil novecientas noventa y una libras *999.991 pounds*

Spanish separates thousands with a full point. The comma is used instead of a decimal point.

5,6 = cinco coma seis   *five point six*

C Round numbers involving **millón**, **millones**, etc. are followed by **de**: un millón de habitantes *one million inhabitants*, but not otherwise: un millón doscientos mil euros *one million two hundred thousand euro*.

Spanish counts in thousands, not hundreds, even with dates where no punctuation is used: 1999 (el año) mil novecientos noventa y nueve.

D Telephone numbers are either given as separate digits, as in English, or more usually divided into convenient groups: 232 24 56 89: (el) doscientos treinta y dos, veinticuatro, cincuenta y seis, ochenta y nueve.

exercise

You are explaining these statistics for a model of car to a Spanish friend. State the figures in words.

a Motor: 1.984 centímetros cuadrados (*cc*)

b Potencia (*power*): 150 C (**caballos** (*horsepower*)) a 6.000 revoluciones

c Neumáticos (*tyres*): 195

d Dimensiones exteriores: 3,85/1,64/1,41 metros

e Velocidad (*speed*) máxima: 216 kilómetros por hora

f Aceleración 0–1 kilómetro: 30,4 segundos

g Consumo: 9 litros en 100 kilómetros

h Precio: 18.000 euros

A summary of days, months, seasons and other time expressions.

A Spanish normally writes days and months with a small letter.

Los días de la semana *Days of the week*

lunes	*Monday*	viernes	*Friday*
martes	*Tuesday*	sábado	*Saturday*
miércoles	*Wednesday*	domingo	*Sunday*
jueves	*Thursday*		
Hoy es lunes.	*Today is Monday.*		

B The definite article (**el / los**) is used for *on*; **los** is used for repeated occasions: el lunes *on Monday*; los lunes *on Mondays*.

Vamos al cine los domingos.   *We go to the cinema on Sundays.*

C Time of day: por la mañana *in the morning*; por la tarde *in the afternoon / evening*; por la noche *during the night*; por la madrugada *in the early morning*.

Salimos el martes por la   *We are leaving on Tuesday*
mañana.   *morning.*

D **Los meses del año** *Months of the year*

enero	abril	julio	octubre
febrero	mayo	agosto	noviembre
marzo	junio	septiembre	diciembre

Voy de vacaciones en agosto.   *I go on holiday in August.*

E To give the date, Spanish uses the order day, month, year.

Es el dos de mayo de mil novecientos noventa y nueve.	*It's the second of May, 1999.*
martes trece	*Tuesday 13th*
el uno de enero / el primero de enero	*1st January*
¿Cuál es la fecha? / ¿Qué fecha es?	*What's the date?*
¿A cuántos estamos hoy?	*What is today's date?*
Estamos a diez de mayo.	*It's the tenth of May.*

F In letters, the town of the sender is usually included as a heading.

Madrid, 28 de febrero de 2003   *Madrid, 28 February 2003*

G Las cuatro estaciones *The four seasons*

primavera	*spring*	otoño	*autumn*
verano	*summer*	invierno	*winter*

exercise

Write the family birthdays in full.

E.g. Madre (1/X) → primero/uno de octubre

a Tío Pepe (22/V)

b Hermana Luisa (18/I)

c Gemelos (*twins*) (5/VIII)

d Hijo (6/III)

e Hija (8/IV)

f Raúl (30/IX)

g Luisa (15/II)

h Abuela (9/XII)

Telling the time in Spanish is very much like in English.

A ¿Qué hora es? *What time is it?*

Es la una.	*It's one o'clock.*
Son las dos.	*It's two o'clock.*
Son las tres, cuatro, cinco, etc.	*It's three o'clock*, etc.

La and **las** are used, as **hora** and **horas** are understood.

B y media *half past*

Son las cinco y media.   *It's half past five.*

• **y cuarto / menos cuarto** *quarter past/quarter to*

Son las seis menos cuarto.	*It's a quarter to six.*
Es la una y cuarto.	*It's a quarter past one.*

Take care to distinguish **cuatro** *four* and **cuarto** *quarter*.

C Minutes past or to the hour are introduced with **y** or **menos**.

Son las cinco y diez.	*It's ten past five.*
Son las cuatro menos veinte.	*It's twenty to four.*

• With odd numbers of minutes, **minutos** is added for clarity, as in English.

Son las cinco y seis minutos.   *It's six minutes past five.*

• **y pico** *just past*; **menos algo** *just before*; **pasadas** *gone*

Son las cinco y pico.	*It's just after five.*
Son las doce menos algo.	*It's coming up to twelve.*
Son las cuatro pasadas.	*It's gone four.*

D To say *At what time?*, Spanish uses **a**.

¿A qué hora sales?   *(At) what time are you going out?*

A las cinco en punto.   *At five, sharp.*

With specific time by the clock, use **de la mañana** for *a.m.*, **de la tarde** or **de la noche** for *p.m.* and **de la madrugada** for the early morning.

¡Son las tres de la madrugada!   *It's three a.m.!*

NB Mi reloj está adelantado / atrasado *My watch is fast / slow.*

exercise

Say what time these clocks show.

a 10.20 a.m.   **b** 2.05 p.m.   **c** 8.45 a.m.

d 11.30 a.m.   **e** just past 1.00 p.m.   **f** almost 9.00 p.m.

Ordinal numbers like *first*, *second* and *third* are less commonly used in Spanish than in English. Nevertheless this unit deals with the important ones.

A Ordinal numbers are generally used only up to *tenth* in Spanish. After that the cardinal numbers are used.

primero	*first*	séptimo	*seventh*
segundo	*second*	octavo	*eighth*
tercero	*third*	noveno	*ninth*
cuarto	*fourth*	décimo	*tenth*
quinto	*fifth*		
sexto	*sixth*	último	*last*

Abbreviations such as 1°, 6ª mean **primero**, **sexta**, etc.

B **Primero** and **tercero** shorten to **primer** and **tercer** in front of a masculine singular noun.

el tercer hombre	*the third man*
la última página	*the last page*
Enrique octavo	*Henry VIII*
el siglo diecinueve	*the nineteenth century*
Luisa vive en el piso doce.	*Luisa lives on the twelfth floor.*

Note Spanish word order in expressions involving ordinals: las tres primeras páginas *the first three pages*; los cinco últimos días *the last five days*.

C For times with travel, transport, entertainment, Spanish uses the 24-hour clock, with minutes counted from one to 59.

El tren sale a las veinte treinta y cinco.

The train leaves at 20.35 (8.35 p.m.).

El concierto empieza a las veintidós (horas) y termina a las veintitrés quince.

The concert starts at 22.00 (10 p.m.) and ends at 23.15 (11.15 p.m.).

exercise

Practise ordinals by reading the following out loud.

a Enrique VIII
b Carlos V
c Juan XXIII
d Alfonso XIII
e Juan Carlos I

f el piso 1°
g el piso 3°
h el siglo VII
i el piso XI
j el siglo XX

Spanish uses different words for time in different contexts.

A **La hora** *time* (clock)

Use **la hora** when you are asking for time by the clock.

¿Qué hora es?	*What time is it?*
¿A qué hora empieza el partido de fútbol?	*(At) what time does the football match start?*

Spanish always requires **a** in such expressions.

B **El tiempo** *time* (abstract sense)

No tengo tiempo para estudiar.	*I don't have time to study.*
Llevo aquí mucho tiempo esperándola.	*I have been waiting here for her for a long time.*
¿Cómo pasan el tiempo aquí?	*How do they pass / spend the time here?*
¿Qué pasatiempos tienes?	*What hobbies / pastimes do you have?*
Hace mucho tiempo había osos en la montañas.	*A long time ago there were bears in the mountains.*

C **El tiempo** can also refer to the weather. The context makes the meaning clear.

¿Qué tiempo hace?	*What's the weather like?*
Hace mal tiempo.	*The weather is bad.*

D **La vez** *time* (number of times)

La última vez que estuve aquí perdí mi dinero.	*The last time I was here I lost my money.*

Te lo digo por última vez.   *I'm telling you for the last time.*

Lo digo sólo una vez.   *I'll say it only once.*

Me llamaron dos veces.   *They rang me twice.*

Note also: muchas veces *often*; pocas veces *seldom*; raras veces *hardly ever, rarely*; a veces *at times, sometimes*; algunas veces *sometimes*.

Raras veces vamos a España.   *We rarely go to Spain.*

The definite article is omitted after **por.**

por primera vez   *for the first time*
por última vez   *for the last time*

exercise

Put in the correct word from the box.

a ¿Qué .... es?

b ¿Qué .... hace?

c ¿A qué ... sale el tren?

d Hace mal ... en diciembre.

e ¿Cuántas .... has visitado Madrid?

f Estoy aquí por primera ... .

g Comemos en un restaurante muchas .... .

h No tenemos .... para descansar.

---

tiempo   hora   veces   tiempo   tiempo   hora   vez   veces

Adjectives are words that describe nouns, for example *green tree*, *tall man*, *the house is big*.

A Adjectives in Spanish agree with the noun to which they refer in gender (masculine or feminine) and number (singular or plural).

Adjectives which end in **-o** change to **-a** (feminine singular), **-os** (masculine plural) and **-as** (feminine plural).

	singular	plural
masculine	un libro pequeño *a small book*	libros pequeños *small books*
feminine	una casa pequeña *a small house*	casas pequeñas *small houses*

B Adjectives agree even when separated from the noun.
La casa es pequeña.   *The house is small.*
Los libros son pequeños.   *The books are small.*

C Not all adjectives have separate feminine forms.

- Adjectives ending in **-e** have no separate feminine form: María está triste. *María is sad.*

- Most adjectives ending in a consonant have no separate feminine form: una falda azul *a blue skirt*

D Adjectives ending in **-or** and most in **-ón** do, however, have feminine forms. Those in **-ón** drop the accent:

Su esposa es mandona.　　*His wife is bossy.*

NB Marrón *brown* has no feminine form.

las botas marrones　　*the brown boots*

E Adjectives of nationality, like **español** *Spanish*, **inglés** *English*, **francés** *French* and **alemán** *German* do have feminine forms. Any final accent is dropped before such endings.

las mujeres inglesas　　*the English women*

Esta revista es alemana.　　*This magazine is German.*

F Most adjectives come after the noun in Spanish.

Aquí hay parques magníficos.　　*There are magnificent parks here.*

exercise

Give the Spanish for the following.

a a pretty girl

b the pretty girls

c The house is white.

d The houses are white.

e The women are English.

f The magazine is Spanish

g Ana is hardworking.

h Luisa and María are hardworking.

i Kylie is Australian.

j The girls are Spanish.

This unit continues a summary of the use of adjectives.

In Unit 16 we saw that adjectives in Spanish usually come after the noun: la casa blanca *the white house*.

A Some adjectives regularly go before the noun, as in English.

- Adjectives showing quantity usually go before. These include **mucho** *much, many*; **poco** *little, few*; **varios** *several*; **algunos** *some*; **bastante/suficiente** *enough*; **ambos** *both* and numbers: muchos libros *many books*; bastante vino *enough wine*; poco dinero *little money*; varias casas *several houses*; dos chicas *two girls*.

- Adjectives can go before the noun if they state a natural characteristic: la blanca nieve *the white snow*.

- Subjective judgements similarly put the adjective first: Es una buena película. *It's a good film.*

- If the adjective comes after an expression with **qué**, Spanish adds **más** *more* or **tan** *such*.
  ¡Qué chica más bonita! ⎫
  ¡Qué chica tan bonita! ⎭ *What a pretty girl!*

B A few adjectives are shortened when they come before the noun. This usually happens only in the masculine singular.

un libro bueno →	un buen libro	*a good book*
un vino malo →	un mal vino	*a bad wine*
el capítulo primero →	el primer capítulo	*the first chapter*
el hombre tercero →	el tercer hombre	*the third man*

Alguno *some* and **uno** *one* are also shortened.

¿Hay algún bar por aquí?   *Is there a bar round here?*
Hay un bar en la plaza.   *There's a bar in the square.*

C Some adjectives change meaning according to their position: un pobre hombre *a poor (wretched) man*; un hombre pobre *a poor (penniless) man*; un nuevo coche *a new (different) car*; un coche nuevo *a (brand-)new car*; un gran general *a great general*; un general grande *a tall general*; Gran Bretaña *Great Britain*

NB Grande becomes **gran** in front of any singular noun.

exercise
Translate the following into Spanish.

a We live (**Vivimos**) in a small house.
b There is (**Hay**) a good film on television.
c Some general lives here.
d He is a great man.
e He is a tall man.
f I live in Great Britain.
g The poor boy has no friends (**no tiene amigos**) .
h The poor man has no money (**dinero**).
i The third book is not good.
j The first chapter is bad.

Sometimes you will need to talk about a combination of items which may be of different number and gender.

A Adjectives covering more than one noun of the same gender agree with that gender in the plural.

Tengo muchos amigos y compañeros.	*I have many friends and companions.*
Come patatas y sardinas fritas.	*He is eating fried potatoes and sardines.*

B With nouns of different genders, use masculine plural adjectives.

Lleva botas y calcetines negros.	*He is wearing black boots and socks.*
Hay muchos chicos y chicas.	*There are many boys and girls.*

C Sometimes you may need more than one adjective, for example, *I live in a little white house.* You have a couple of possibilities.

• You can make a 'noun sandwich'. This is common when one adjective customarily comes before the noun.

Vivo en una pequeña casa blanca.	*I live in a little white house*

• The adjectives may be linked with y *and.*

Es una chica inteligente y trabajadora.	*She is an intelligent and hard-working girl.*

NB Remember to change **y** to **e** in front of **i-** or **hi-**.
Es un estudiante trabajador e *He is a hard-working and*
inteligente.   *intelligent student.*

D Compound adjectives like *dark-red* are invariable.
una falda rojo oscuro   *a dark-red skirt*
unos vaqueros azul claro   *light-blue jeans*

E A noun may be used as an invariable adjective.
un coche (color de) naranja   *an orange car*
camisas café   *coffee-coloured shirts*
Éstas son las casas piloto.   *These are the show houses.*
unos coches modelo   *model cars*

exercise

Fill the gaps with appropriate adjectives taken from the box.

Vivo en un **a** _____ pueblo **b** _____ con **c** _____ casas
d _____. Las casas tienen jardines **e** _____ y **f** _____ con
rosas **g** _____ y violetas **h** _____. En mi jardín hay unas
rosas especiales – son **i** _____ y son muy **j** _____. Los
habitantes visitan mi jardín porque son muy **k** _____ y
quieren ver esta rosa **l** _____.

| amarillas | azul claro | azules | bonito | bonitos | curiosos |
| diferente | grandes | muchas | pequeño | raras | viejas |

Adverbs are used to describe actions and in English often end in *-ly* like *deeply, loudly, slowly*. In a similar way, Spanish adds *-mente* to the corresponding adjective.

alegre → alegremente *happily*   triste → tristemente *sadly*

A The adjective and **-mente** were originally considered as separate words, so any accent on the basic adjective is retained when it becomes an adverb.

fácil → fácilmente *easily*

B Adjectives which have a separate feminine form add **-mente** to this.

lento / lenta → lentamente *slowly*
serio / seria → seriamente *seriously*
rápido / rápida → rápidamente *quickly*

When Spanish has a string of adverbs, only the final one takes **-mente**, though feminine singular adjectives are used in anticipation of **-mente**.

Juan sirve rápida, seria y   *Juan serves quickly,*
  amablemente.   *seriously and kindly.*

C A few adverbs are special forms:

bueno *good* → bien *well*   malo *bad* → mal *badly*.

D Some adverbs are identical to the adjective: mejor *better*; peor *worse*; mucho *a lot*; poco *a little / little*; tarde *late*; temprano *early*; más *more*; menos *less*; demasiado *too (much)*; bastante *enough*.

Usted habla demasiado.   *You talk too much.*

E • **Más**, **menos**, **demasiado** and **bastante** can be used as intensifiers with other adverbs.

Hable menos rápidamente.	*Speak less quickly.*
Juan canta bastante bien.	*Juan sings quite well.*

• **Muy** *very* can also be used to modify adverbs.

Luisa habla muy precisamente.	*Luisa speaks very precisely.*

• The adjective **tanto** *so much* becomes **tan** (*so*).

Mantenga limpia España – es tan bonita.	*Keep Spain tidy – it's so pretty.*

• When **alto / fuerte** and **bajo** are used figuratively with the meaning of *loudly* and *softly*, the unchanged adjective form is kept.

Hable alto.	*Speak loudly.*

exercise

Form adverbs from the following adjectives.

E.g. alegre → alegremente.

a diferente	**i** inteligente	**q** lento
b difícil	**j** cruel	**r** nervioso
c fácil	**k** evidente	**s** calmo
d formal	**l** responsable	**t** tranquilo
e natural	**m** raro	**u** serio
f elegante	**n** rápido	**v** franco
g mayor	**o** claro	**w** divino
h principal	**p** estupendo	**x** furioso

In English, we use words like *more* or *less* to compare quantities. This unit deals with comparisons in Spanish.

A To say *more than* or *less than*, use **más que** and **menos que**.

Tengo más dinero que Julio.	*I have more money than Julio.*
Julia bebe más vino que cerveza.	*Julia drinks more wine than beer.*
Tenemos menos tiempo que tú.	*We've less time than you.*
Julio trabaja más que Ignacio.	*Julio works harder than Ignacio.*

B However, if *more than* or *less than* refers only to quantity, use **más de** and **menos de**.

Bebe más de dos litros de vino.	*He drinks more than two litres of wine.*
Trabajamos menos de dos horas al día.	*We work less than two hours per day.*

Luisa come más que un hombre.   Luisa come más de un hombre.

C If the comparison is with an abstract, use **más / menos de lo que**.

Cuesta más de lo que piensa.   *It costs more than he thinks.*
Me duele menos de lo que   *It hurts less than I expected.*
esperaba.

Note also the use of **del que, de la que, de los que, de las que** agreeing with specific nouns.

Tiene más dinero del que dice.   *He / She has more money*
    than he / she says.

Tiene más cerveza de la que   *He / She has more beer*
dice.   *than he / she says.*

Tiene más libros de los que dice.   *He / She has more books*
    than he / she says.

Tiene más revistas de las que   *He / She has more magazines*
dice.   *than he / she says.*

D To say that two comparisons are the same, use **tanto como** and make the **tanto** agree with the object referred to.

Tengo tanta cerveza como   *I have as much beer as*
Julio.   *Julio.*

Tengo tantas revistas como   *I have as many magazines*
Julio.   *as Julio.*

With an adjective or adverb, **tanto** becomes **tan**.

Soy tan inteligente como   *I am as intelligent as*
Ignacio.   *Ignacio.*

Leo tan rápidamente como tú.   *I read as quickly as you.*

See exercise 12 in 'More practice'.

21 comparisons (2)

This unit looks at the comparative forms of adjectives and adverbs like *prettier*, *more quickly*, *as clearly*.

A Más / menos with adjectives

- Superiority is indicated by **más** + adjective + **que**.

La ciudad es más bonita que la playa.	*The town is prettier than the beach.*
Las chicas aquí son más guapas que en mi pueblo.	*The girls here are more beautiful than in my village.*

- Adverbs are compared in the same way.

Juan escribe más rápidamente que Luisa.	*Juan writes more quickly Luisa.*

- Inferiority is likewise shown using **menos**.

La playa es menos bonita que la ciudad.	*The beach is less pretty than the town.*
Luisa escribe menos claramente que Juan.	*Luisa writes less clearly than Juan.*

- Similarity is shown using **tan** + adjective / adverb + **como**.

Luisa escribe tan claramente como Catalina.	*Luisa writes as clearly as Catalina.*

B Just as English has some irregular forms like *better*, so does Spanish: mejor *better*; peor *worse*; mayor *older*, *more important*; menor *younger*, *less important*; superior *upper*; inferior *lower*.

NB These adjectives have no separate feminine form.

El libro es mejor que la *The book is better than the*
película. *film.*

C To say *even (worse)* etc., use **aun**.

La película es aun peor que *The film is even worse than*
la novela. *the novel.*

D **Mejor** and **peor** can be used as adverbs.

Tú hablas español mejor *You speak Spanish better*
que yo. *than I do.*

The forms **más bueno** and **más malo** usually refer to moral
qualities; **más grande** and **menos grande** refer to physical size,
whereas **mayor** and **menor** refer to age or status.

Madrid es más grande que *Madrid is bigger than*
Sevilla. *Seville.*

exercise

Join sentences to make one, comparing the three descriptions.

E.g. **Luisa es inteligente. Julio. Yo** → **Luisa es más inteligente
que Julio pero menos inteligente que yo.**

a Barcelona es grande. Sevilla. Madrid.

b Carlos es valiente. Federico. Juan.

c Luisa conduce rápidamente. Mi hermana. Julia.

d Paco canta bien. Miguel. Julio.

This time, practise using *tan(to)* como using the same prompts.

E.g. **Luisa es tan inteligente como Julio pero no es tan
inteligente como yo.**

We see superlatives around us every day, especially in adverbs: the *whitest* wash of all, the *best* lemonade in the world, the *most expensive* ingredients and so on.

A The good news is that superlatives in Spanish are very similar to the comparative forms, except that you add the definite article (**el, la, los, las**) or a possessive ajective (**mi, tu,** etc.).

COMPARATIVE

Quiero ver un deporte más peligroso.	*I want to watch a more dangerous sport.*

SUPERLATIVE

Quiero ver el deporte más peligroso del mundo.	*I want to watch the most dangerous sport in the world.*

NB **Éste es mi mejor amigo.** *This is my best friend.*

B After a superlative, use **de** to translate *in*.

Luis es el estudiante más inteligente de la clase.	*Luis is the most intelligent student in the class.*

C Another way is to form an 'absolute superlative', by adding **-ísimo** to the basic adjective. This often has the force in English of *ever so ...* or *extremely*.

Luisa es guapísima.	*Luisa is ever so good-looking.*
Este pueblo es feísimo.	*This little town is extremely ugly.*

You will have to watch your spelling rules.

ri<u>c</u>o → riqu<u>í</u>simo   lar<u>g</u>o → largu<u>í</u>simo

feliz (*happy*) - feli<u>c</u>ísimo   elegant<u>e</u> → elegant<u>í</u>simo

dif<u>í</u>cil → dif<u>í</u>cilísimo

-ísimo always needs an accent.

D Adverbs usually form their superlatives with **muy** *very* or **extremadamente** *extremely*.

Juan trabaja extremadamente   *Juan works extremely hard.*
  duro.

Hablan muy rápidamente.   *They speak very quickly.*

E **Muchísimo** *very much*; **poquísimo** *very little*

Los chicos estudian muchísimo   *The boys are working*
  para el examen.   *very hard for the exam.*

Aquí la gente trabaja   *Here, people work very*
  poquísimo.   *little.*

exercise

You've had enough! Complain about your treatment. Use *más* or *menos* as necessary.

E.g. habitación sucia hotel → **Tengo la habitación más sucia del hotel.**

a coche viejo compañía   **g** dentista simpático pueblo

b asiento malo teatro   **h** día aburrido fábrica

c secretaria trabajadora oficina   **i** vacaciones largas colegio

d colega hablador departamento   **j** plato asqueroso

e esposa fea mundo   restaurante

f dolor terrible todo

Demonstratives are words that show or point out something, like *this*, *that*, *those* and *these*.

A Demonstrative adjectives agree in gender and number with the nouns to which they refer, and they normally go in front of the noun.

There are three demonstrative adjectives in Spanish. In addition to **este** *this*, it distinguishes between **ese** *that near you* and **aquel** *that over there*.

masc. sing.	este	ese	aquel
masc. pl.	estos	esos	aquellos
fem. sing.	esta	esa	aquella
fem. pl.	estas	esas	aquellas

B When the demonstratives stand on their own, an accent is placed on the stressed syllable to show that they are pronouns.

- **éste, ésta, éstos, éstas** *this one, these ones*
  Mi casa es ésta – éstas son   *My house is this (one) –*
  mis hermanas.   *these are my sisters.*

- **ése, ésa, ésos, ésas** *that one, those ones*
  ¿Qué revista es ésa?   *What magazine is that (one)?*

- **aquél, aquélla, aquéllos, aquéllas** *that one, those ones*
  ¿Qué montañas son aquéllas?   *What mountains are those?*

C Esto, eso, aquello

If something has not yet been identified, so consequently has not been given a gender, use these neuter pronouns.

¿Qué es eso? ¡Es horrible!   *What's that? It's horrible!*

NB Esto, eso and **aquello** never take an accent and are never used as adjectives.

exercise

Put in the demonstrative adjective or pronoun as necessary.

E.g. (este) casa es grande → Esta casa es grande.

(este) es la casa de mi amigo → Ésta es la casa de mi amigo.

a (aquel) chicos son inteligentes.
b ¿Qué estudiantes son (aquel)?
c ¿Qué es (aquel)? ¿Es carne?
d (este) chica es muy bonita.
e (esta) es mi hermana.
f (aquel) montañas son bonitas.
g ¿Qué montañas son (aquel)?
h ¿Qué es (este)?
i ¿Qué chica es (ese)?
j ¿De quién es (aquel) falda?

Possessive adjectives indicate ownership and correspond to _my, your, his_, etc. in English.

A Possessive adjectives come before the noun. Like other adjectives in Spanish, they agree in gender and number with the noun to which they refer.

	_my_	_your_ (fam.)	_his, her_ _your_ (pol.)	_our_	_your_ (fam.)	_their, your_ (pol.)
masc. sing.	mi	tu	su	nuestro	vuestro	su
masc. pl.	mis	tus	sus	nuestros	vuestros	sus
fem. sing.	mi	tu	su	nuestra	vuestra	su
fem. pl.	mis	tus	sus	nuestras	vuestras	sus

mi libro _my book_, tus libros _your books_, sus casas _his / her / your / their houses_, nuestra casa _our house_, vuestros libros _your books_

B To avoid ambiguity, since **su** can mean _his, her, their, your_ (singular polite) and _your_ (plural polite), you can specify who the **su** refers to by adding **de él, de ella, de ellos, de ellas, de usted** or **de ustedes**: su coche de usted _your car_

You can also say simply **la casa de usted**, etc.

The possessive adjectives agree with the thing possessed, not the person who owns it. Hence **su casa** means _his, her, their, your house_ and **sus casas** means _his, her, their, your houses._

exercise

Correct the possessive adjectives.

E.g. ¿Es el libro de Julio? (*our*) → No, es nuestro libro.

a ¿Es el coche de Juan? (*my*)

b ¿Es el vino de Juanita? (*your (familiar)*)

c ¿Es la revista de Julio? (*her*)

d ¿Son las botas de Pedro? (*our*)

e ¿Son los periódicos de Ana? (*their (feminine)*)

Possessive pronouns are words like *mine* and *yours*, which refer to a noun or nouns already identified.

Su coche es blanco pero el
mío es azul.

*His car is white but mine is
blue.*

A Possessive pronouns agree in gender and number with the noun they represent.

	singular		plural	
	masculine	feminine	masculine	feminine
mine	el mío	la mía	los míos	las mías
yours (fam.)	el tuyo	la tuya	los tuyos	las tuyas
his, hers yours (pol.)	el suyo	la suya	los suyos	las suyas
ours	el nuestro	la nuestra	los nuestros	las nuestras
yours (fam.)	el vuestro	la vuestra	los vuestros	las vuestras
theirs, yours (pol.)	el suyo	la suya	los suyos	las suyas

Éste es mi vino, ¿dónde está
el tuyo?

*This is my wine, where is
yours?*

Nuestros padres trabajan mucho
pero los suyos trabajan poco.

*Our parents work hard
but his work little.*

B El suyo may be clarified with de él, de usted, etc.

Mi revista es ésta – ¿Cuál es la (suya) de usted?	*This is my magazine – which is yours?*

C With names, use el de, la de, los de, las de + the name.

mi coche y el de Julio	*my car and Julio's*
nuestras botas y las de Ana y Pedro	*our boots and Ana and Pedro's*

D After ser *to be*, possessive pronouns usually drop the definite article.

Este libro es mío – aquél es tuyo.	*This book is mine – that one is yours.*
Esta habitación es nuestra.	*This room is ours.*

E The long forms of the possessives like mío, etc., may occasionally be used as adjectives but must come after the noun.

¡Dios mío!	*My God!*

Note also expressions like un amigo mío *a friend of mine*.

Muy Señor mío *Dear Sir* (in formal letters).

See exercise 14 in 'More practice'.

Subject pronouns (*I*, *you*, *he*, etc.) are not used as frequently in Spanish as in English, as the verb ending itself usually makes clear who the subject is. They may, however, be included for clarity or emphasis.

> Tú trabajas mucho pero yo prefiero dormir.
>
> *You work hard but I prefer to sleep.*

A The personal pronouns are first, second or third person.

	singular	plural
1st person	yo *I*	nosotros/nosotras *we*
2nd person	tú *you* (familiar)	vosotros/vosotras *you* (familiar)
3rd person	él *he* ella *she* usted *you* (formal)	ellos *they* (masculine) ellas *they* (feminine) ustedes *you* (formal)

B Yo is written with a small letter except as the first word of a sentence.

> Yo soy profesor. El profesor, soy yo. *I'm a teacher. The teacher – that's me.*

C Nosotros, vosotros and ellos distinguish gender: **nosotras somos alumnas** (*we* (girls) *are pupils*). As all Spanish nouns are masculine or feminine, **él, ella, ellos** and **ellas** refer also to things, not just people.

D Spanish has four forms for *you* to distinguish degrees of familiarity and number. **Tú** and **vosotros** are singular and plural and express familiarity – family, friends, close colleagues. They are used with second-person verb endings, singular and plural as appropriate. **Usted** and **ustedes** are used to express formality or politeness. They are always used with third-person verb endings (like extremely formal English *How is Your Majesty? How are Your Excellencies?*)

¿Cómo está usted, señor?	*How are you, sir?*
¿Cómo están ustedes, señoras y señores?	*How are you, ladies and gentlemen?*

E **Usted** and **ustedes** are often written **Vd.** and **Vds.** (**Ud.** and **Uds.** are also used, particularly in America). Outside of Spain, **vosotros** can sound old-fashioned or has religious, poetic overtones. In America (and in some parts of southern Spain) **ustedes** is used for the plural *you* in all cases.

exercise

Add personal subject pronouns for emphasis.

E.g. _____ bebo → yo bebo

a _____ trabajo.

b _____ trabajamos.

c ¿_____ trabajáis, chicos?

d ¿Dónde están _____ , señores?

e _____ es española pero _____ es inglés.

f ¿Cómo está _____ , señora?

Disjunctive pronouns are used after prepositions.

They are used in both English and Spanish in such expressions as *for him, without us, from them*. All disjunctive means is that the pronoun is separated (dis-joined) from the verb.

A The good news is that most disjunctive pronouns in Spanish are the same as the subject pronouns.

Tengo un regalo para él y para ella.	*I have a present for him and for her.*
Una botella de vino para nosotros y champán para ustedes.	*A bottle of wine for us and champagne for you.*

B The bad news is that **yo** changes to **mí** and **tú** changes to **ti** after a preposition. Note that **mí** has an accent, but **ti** does not.

¿Es la carta para mí o para ti?	*Is the letter for me or for you?*

After some prepositions, the ordinary subject pronouns are used instead of **mí** and **ti**. These include **según yo** *according to me*, **entre tú y yo** *between you and me*, **salvo, excepto, menos** *except*.

Todos excepto yo.	*Everyone except me.*

C To summarize, disjunctive pronouns are as follows.

	singular	plural
1st person	(para) mí	(para) nosotros/nosotras
2nd person	(para) ti	(para) vosotros/vosotras
3rd person	(para) él (para) ella (para) usted	(para) ellos (para) ellas (para) ustedes

D Conmigo *with me*, contigo *with you*, consigo *with oneself*

The preposition **con** *with* combines with **mí** and **ti** to create two special forms, **conmigo** and **contigo**.

¿Quieres ir conmigo?	*Do you want to go with me?*
Siempre quiero estar contigo.	*I always want to be with you.*

Consigo *with oneself* is used with any third person to refer back to the same subject.

Juan lleva mucho dinero consigo.	*Juan takes a lot of money with him.*
Ustedes traen la comida consigo.	*You bring the food with you.*

See exercise 15 in 'More practice'.

**Direct object pronouns are words like *it*, *them*, *me*, *us*, *him*
which replace nouns.**

A In English, we put object pronouns after the verb: *I eat it*;
they know us, etc. Spanish normally places the object pronoun
in front of the verb: **lo como** *I eat it*; **nos conocen** *they know
us*.

B Spanish object pronouns reflect the gender and number of
the noun being replaced.

	Singular	Plural
1st person	me	nos
2nd person	te	os
3rd person	lo / la	los (*masculine*) / las (*feminine*)

¿Dónde está el chocolate? No
  lo veo.
(**lo** = **el chocolate**)

*Where is the chocolate? I
don't see it.*

No veo la cerveza – ¿la has
  bebido?
(**la** = **la cerveza**)

*I don't see the beer, have
you drunk it?*

C **lo**, **la**, **los** and **las** refer to both people and things. In
educated usage in Spain, many people use **le** rather than **lo** to
refer to a masculine, singular person.
  Le conozco. / Lo conozco.   *I know him.*

Usted and ustedes, the polite words for *you,* are third-person pronouns, so the corresponding direct object forms are also lo, la, los and las.

La conozco, María.	*I know you, María.*
¿Los señores de López? ¡No los vi!	*Mr and Mrs López – I didn't see you!*

D To make the expression negative, **no** comes in front of the object pronoun but after any subject.

Yo no te conozco.	*I don't know you.*
No te he visto nunca.	*I've never seen you.*

E When two verbs are used together, for example, *I am going to buy it,* the object pronoun goes either in front of the first verb or is added to the infinitive to make one word, but NEVER goes between the verbs.

Lo voy a comprar. / Voy a comprarlo.	*I'm going to buy it.*
Queremos verlos. / Los queremos ver.	*We want to see them.*

exercise

Use object pronouns instead of the nouns.

E.g. ¿Quieres el libro? → Lo tengo.

a ¿Quieres la cerveza?

b ¿Quieres los cigarrillos?

c ¿Quieres las patatas?

d ¿Quieres pan?

e ¿Quieres mucho dinero?

Indirect objects are words like *(to) him, (to) me*, that show the recipient of a verb.

A In English, the indirect pronouns are sometimes introduced with *to*: *I show the book to him* (*I show him the book*). Spanish does not require a preposition: **le muestro el libro, me da el libro.**

B As with the direct object pronouns (see Unit 28), Spanish usually places the indirect object in front of the verb.

	singular	plural
1st person	me *(to) me*	nos *(to) us*
2nd person	te *(to) you*	os *(to) you*
3rd person	le *(to) him, her, you*	les *(to) them, you*

You can see that the first and second persons are the same as the direct object pronouns. In the third person **le** and **les** are used for either gender.

Le doy el libro.   *I give him / her / you* (polite)
                                 the book.

Les doy el libro.   *I give them / you* (plural)
                                 the book.

C If there is any ambiguity, you can clarify who the **le/les** refers to by adding **a** with a disjunctive pronoun (see Unit 27): **a él, a ella, a usted, a ellos, a ellas, a ustedes,** but you still keep the **le / les** as well!

Le doy el libro a usted.   *I give the book to you.*
No les hablo a ustedes.   *I'm not talking to you.*

When two verbs come together, the same word order as with
direct object pronouns applies.

Quiero decirle la verdad. /   *I want to tell him/her/you*
  Le quiero decir la verdad.   *the truth.*

D When two object pronouns come together, any first person
takes precedence over a second or third person.

Me lo presenta.   *He is presenting it to me.*

E With two third-person object pronouns, the indirect comes
in front of the direct. The first **le** or **les** changes to **se**.

Se lo entrego.   *I'm handing it to him / her/*
                       you / them.

F With two object pronouns tacked on the end of an
infinitive, an accent is always needed to maintain the stress.

No voy a decírselo.   *I'm not going to say it to*
                     him, etc.

exercise

Put the supplied object pronouns in the correct order.

a dice (lo, me)
b quiero hablar (le)
c No puedo decir (te, lo)
d entregamos (te, las)
e doy (te, lo)
f presenta (nos, lo)

English has a number of words or expressions beginning with *some-* or *any-*, for example *someone, anybody, something,* to refer to specific but undefined situations.

A algo *something / anything*

¿Quiere usted algo más?	*Do you want anything else?*
Hay algo en el armario.	*There's something in the cupboard.*

Algo can also be used with an adjective to mean *somewhat* or *rather.*

Esto es algo difícil.	*This is rather difficult.*

B alguien *someone*

Hay alguien en la casa.	*There's someone in the house.*
¿Conoces a alguien aquí?	*Do you know anyone here?*

Alguien takes a personal **a** (see Unit 94).

C alguno *some*

Like **uno**, **alguno** agrees with the noun.

Luisa conoce algunas ciudades de América.	*Luisa knows some cities in America.*
Alguna gente prefiere dormir.	*Some people prefer to sleep.*
Juan trabaja en algún colegio en Madrid.	*Juan is working in some school in Madrid.*

Alguno becomes **algún** in front of a masculine singular noun.

D alguna parte *somewhere*

Vive en alguna parte del sur.   *He lives somewhere in the south.*

Hay servicios por alguna parte aquí.   *There are toilets somewhere round here.*

E cualquiera *any one*

¿Qué libro quieres? Cualquiera.   *Which book do you want? Any (one).*

Cualquiera puede hacerlo.   *Anyone can do it.*

Cualquiera becomes **cualquier** in front of any singular noun and **cualesquier** in front of any plural noun.

El tren sale en cualquier momento.   *The train is leaving at any moment.*

Se venden en cualesquier tiendas.   *They are sold in any shops.*

exercise

Fill the blanks with the appropriate indefinite word from the box.

a Para mí la ópera es _____ interesante.

b Hay _____ en mi habitación – ¿eres tú, Julio?

c _____ gente piensa que el vino es malo.

d Necesito _____ más – un kilo de patatas.

e La conocí en _____ .

algo	algo	alguien	alguna	alguna parte

You can't always agree to everything, so you need to learn how to say *no*!

A The simplest way is to put **no** in front of the verb.

Hablo español pero no hablo portugués.

I speak Spanish but I don't speak Portuguese.

B **No** comes after any subject pronoun but before any reflexive or object pronoun.

Yo no te escucho.   *I'm not listening to you.*

Usted no se levanta tarde.   *You don't get up late.*

C **Nunca** *never* is used in the same way.

Tú nunca me ayudas.   *You never help me.*

Yo nunca bebo cerveza.   *I never drink beer.*

No vuelvo allí nunca jamás.   *I'm never ever going back there.*

D Unlike English, Spanish allows (indeed requires) two or more negative words in the same expression.

Nadie nunca hace nada.   *No one ever does anything.*

If a negative word comes after the verb, Spanish requires **no** or another negative word in front.

Nadie trabaja aquí. /   *No one works here.*
No trabaja aquí nadie.

Do not add **no** if a negative word is already present before the verb.

Nadie aquí habla español.   *No one here speaks Spanish.*

E **Nadie** used as the object of a verb requires personal **a**.
No conozco a nadie aquí.   *I don't know anyone here.*

F **Ninguno** is the corresponding negative form of **alguno** (*some*).
No hay ningunas entradas para   *There are no tickets for the*
el concierto.   *concert.*

Ninguno becomes **ningún** in front of a masculine singular noun.
No he visto ningún hotel.   *I haven't seen any hotel.*

Note that **alguno** used after a negative verb and placed after its noun has an emphatic but negative meaning.

No hay remedio alguno.   *There's no alternative at all.*

exercise

Answer these questions in the negative.

E.g. Tú siempre bebes vino. → Yo nunca bebo vino.

a Yo siempre como patatas.
b Juan llega tarde con frecuencia.
c Alguien me ha ayudado en la casa.
d Algún español vive aquí.
e Mucho es interesante aquí.
f Alguna chica trabaja mucho.

In Unit 31 we saw that Spanish allows more than one negative word in one expression. Here are some more you may need.

A ni … ni … *neither … nor …*

Yo no tengo ni casa ni dinero.	*I have neither house nor money.*
Ni Juan ni Pedro me ayuda nunca.	*Neither Juan nor Pedro ever helps me.*

B tampoco *neither*

Tú no comes pescado – yo tampoco.	*You don't eat fish – me neither.*
Julio no me ayuda tampoco.	*Julio doesn't help me either.*
María tampoco come mariscos.	*María doesn't eat shellfish either.*

C ni siquiera *not even*

No tengo ni siquiera un peso.	*I don't have even a peso.*

D Negative words such as **nada**, **nadie** and **nunca** are needed after **sin** *without*, **antes de / que** *before*, **más / menos que** *more / less than* where English uses *anything, anyone, ever*, etc.

Julio salió sin decir nada.	*Julio went out without saying anything.*
Luisa terminó el examen antes que nadie.	*Luisa finished the exam before anyone.*
Te quiero más que nunca.	*I love you more than ever.*

E Pessimistic expressions like **es imposible** *it's impossible* are also followed by negatives.

Es imposible hacer nada aquí.   *It's impossible to do anything here.*

F **ya no** *no longer*

Ya no fumo.   *I no longer smoke.*
Antes fumaba, pero ya no.   *I used to smoke, but no longer.*

G **todavía no / no ... todavía** *not yet, still not*

Luisa todavía no se ha levantado.
Luisa no se ha levantado   *Luisa has not got up yet.*
todavía.

Todavía can be replaced with **aún.**

Aún no sabía qué hacer.   *I still didn't know what to do.*

NB The expressions **en la vida** and **en absoluto,** which look positive, are emphatic negatives!

En la vida he comido carne.   *I have never eaten meat in my life.*

¿Quieres probar los mariscos?   *Do you want to try the*
En absoluto.   *shellfish? Absolutely not.*

See exercise 17 in 'More practice'.

We use relative pronouns, like *who* or *which*, to make two sentences into one.

Spanish uses **que** *which* and **quien** *who* in a similar way. **Que** and **quien** do not have accents when used as relative pronouns.

A **que** *which, who*

• **Que** can refer to persons or things.

La casa que está en el campo es muy bonita.	*The house which is in the country is very pretty.*
El libro que lees no es muy interesante.	*The book (which) you are reading isn't very interesting.*
La mujer que ves en la foto es española.	*The woman (who/whom) you see in the photo is Spanish.*

English sometimes leaves out the relative pronouns when they refer to the object of the verb. Spanish, however, always includes them.

• **Que** may be used after **a**, **de** and **con** when referring to a thing, but not to a person.

Ésta es la casa de que te hablaba.	*This is the house I was talking to you about.*

In everyday English, we can put words like *to*, *about* and *with* at the end of the sentence: *with which I was writing* → *I was writing with*. This must never be done in Spanish.

B **el cual, la cual** *which*

With other prepositions, **que** is replaced with **el cual, la cual, los cuales** or **las cuales**.

la casa delante de la cual hay un jardín magnífico	*the house in front of which there is a wonderful garden*
los chicos para los cuales compramos los regalos	*the children for whom we bought the presents*

C **quien, quienes** *who, whom*

If the relative pronoun refers to a person, and is the object of verb, **que** can be replaced by **a quien** (**a quienes** if plural).

La mujer a quien conociste en Madrid ha muerto.	*The woman (whom) you met in Madrid has died.*
Los niños a quienes dabas clase ahora viven en otra ciudad.	*The children (whom) you used to teach now live in another town.*

exercise

Join the two sentences into one using *que*.

E.g. El hombre lleva gafas. El hombre trabaja en en jardín.
→ El hombre que trabaja en el jardín lleva gafas.

a La chica es la hermana de Luisa. La chica canta bien.

b El vino no me gusta. El vino se hace aquí.

c La fruta es mala. La fruta se vende en el mercado.

d El libro fue interesante. Me recomendaste el libro.

e El hotel era muy caro. Nos quedamos en el hotel.

We use question words like *how? what? when? where? who?* to request information.

Spanish has a similar set of question words: all are written with an accent on the stressed syllable and are preceded by an upside-down question mark (¿).

A ¿Qué? *What? Which?*

¿Qué es esto?	*What's this?*
¿Qué ciudad es ésta?	*What town is this?*

B ¿Cuál? / ¿Cuáles? *Which?* (identified more closely)

¿Cuál es la ciudad más grande de la región?	*Which is the biggest town in the region?*
¿Cuáles son los platos típicos?	*Which are the typical dishes?*

¿Cuál? and **¿Cuáles?** are not used next to a noun in correct Spanish. Use **¿Qué?** instead.

¿Qué platos son los típicos?	*Which dishes are typical?*

C Qué may be used after a preposition.

¿En qué habitación están ustedes?	*What room are you in?*
¿De qué película hablas?	*What film are you talking about?*
¿Con qué chica sales?	*Which girl are you going out with?*

Unlike everyday English, the preposition must never go at the end of the sentence in Spanish.

D ¿Quién? / ¿Quiénes? *Who?*

| ¿Quién es esa chica? | *Who is that girl?* |
| ¿Quiénes son esas chicas? | *Who are those girls?* |

E ¿A quién? / ¿A quiénes? *Who(m) as a direct object*

| ¿A quién viste allí? | *Who(m) did you see there?* |
| ¿A quiénes quieren? | *Who(m) do they love?* |

F ¿De quién? / ¿De quiénes? *Whose?*

| ¿De quién es este coche? | *Whose car is this?* |
| ¿De quiénes son aquellos coches? | *Whose cars are those?* |

NB Note the different word order in Spanish.

exercise

Ask questions using ¿Qué? ¿Quién? or ¿Quiénes?

E.g. ¿_____ es paella? → ¿Qué es paella?

a ¿_____ son mariscos?
b ¿_____ es el presidente?
c ¿_____ significa esto?
d ¿_____ son los estudiantes?
e ¿_____ es la capital de España?
f ¿_____ libro prefieres?
g ¿_____ es tu mejor amigo?
h ¿_____ son los cantantes?

This unit looks at some more question words.

A ¿Dónde? *Where?*
¿Dónde vive usted?   *Where do you live?*
¿Dónde está la plaza?   *Where is the square?*

¿Adónde? (old English *whither?*), should correctly be used with movement, though this is frequently not observed.
¿Adónde vas?   *Where are you going?*

B ¿Cuándo? *When?*
¿Cuándo piensas casarte?   *When do you intend to get married?*

C ¿Cómo? *How?*
¿Cómo se va a la plaza?   *How does one get to the square?*
¿Cómo está Juan?   *How is Juan?*

With **ser**, ¿cómo? asks *what is* (something/someone) *like?*
¿Cómo es Juan?   *What is Juan like?*

¿Cómo? is used to request repetition or show surprise.
Hoy no hay clase. ¿Cómo?   *There's no lesson today. What?*

D ¿Cuánto? *How much?* agrees with the noun referred to.
¿Cuánta paella quiere?   *How much paella do you want?*
¿Cuántos cigarrillos tienes?   *How many cigarettes do you have?*
¿Cuánto es? / ¿Cuánto vale?   *How much is it?*
¿Cuánto son? ¿Cuánto valen?   *How much are they?*

E **¿Por qué?** *Why? For what reason?*, **¿Para qué?** *Why? For what purpose?*

¿Por qué no puedes ir al cine?   *Why can't you go to the cinema?*

¿Para qué haces eso?   *Why are you doing that?*

Don't forget **¿Por qué?** (two words, accent needed) *Why?* but **porque** (one word, no accent) *because*.

F In reported (or indirect) speech, such as *She asked me what I was doing*, the question word retains the accent: **Me preguntó qué hacía.**

Me dijeron cuántos cigarrillos tenían.   *They told me how many cigarettes they had.*

No sabía dónde vivías.   *I didn't know where you lived.*

exercise

Complete the sentences.

a ¿_____ son las ciudades importantes?

b ¿_____ es paella?

c ¿_____ está Barcelona?

d ¿_____ son los Reyes de España?

e ¿_____ valen las entradas?

f ¿_____ es Granada?

g ¿_____ habitantes tiene?

h ¿_____ día es hoy?

i ¿_____ es el presidente?

j ¿_____ fue el problema?

A conjunction is a word that links elements in a phrase or sentence. Two common English conjunctions are *and* and *or*.

A Y *and*

Julio y Julia hablan español.	*Julio and Julia speak Spanish.*
Julio come pescado y patatas.	*Julio eats fish and potatoes.*
Julio come pescado y Julia come fruta.	*Julio eats fish and Julia eats fruit.*

When **y** comes before a word beginning with **i-** or **hi-**, it is changed to **e**.

Julia e Isabel comen mucho.	*Julia and Isabel eat a lot.*
Madre e hija salen juntas.	*Mother and daughter go out together.*

B O *or*

¿Es usted inglés o español?	*Are you English or Spanish?*
Necesito un bolígrafo o un lápiz.	*I need a biro or a pencil.*
¡Dame el dinero o yo tiro!	*Give me the cash or I'll shoot!*

When **o** comes before a word beginning with **o-** or **ho-**, it is changed to **u**.

Hay diez u once personas en el restaurante.	*There are ten or eleven people in the restaurant*
Busco un restaurante u hotel.	*I'm looking for a restaurant or hotel.*

Between figures, **o** is usually written **ó** for clarity.

100 ó 200 euros	*100 or 200 euro*
22 ó 23	*22 or 23*
en 4 ó 5 días	*in 4 or 5 days*

C Ni *n(or)*

After a negative verb, Spanish uses **ni**.

No tengo dinero ni casa.	*I haven't money or home.*
No bailo ni canto.	*I don't dance or sing.*

You can also say:

No tengo ni amigos ni colegas.	*I have neither friends nor colleagues.*
Ni canto ni bailo.	*I neither dance (n)or sing.*

exercise

Link the expressions with y or e as necessary.

a Juan _____ Ignacio   d padres _____ hijos

b Ignacio _____ Juan   e restaurantes _____ hoteles

c vino _____ aceite   f libertad _____ aire libre

Use o or u as necessary.

g Antonio _____ Octavio

h Octavio _____ Antonio

i siete _____ ocho

j ¿Es septiembre _____ octubre?

k julio _____ agosto

l odio _____ adoro

Spanish has different ways of expressing the conjunction *but*. This unit looks at them and equivalent expressions.

A Pero = *but*

This is used in most cases.

Como mucho pero bebo poco.	*I eat a lot but drink little.*
Dame el dinero, pero si te mueves yo tiro.	*Give me the cash, but if you move I'll shoot.*
Julia trabaja hoy pero está muy enferma.	*Julia is working today but she's very ill.*
No trabajo hoy pero tengo que ir a la oficina.	*I'm not working today but I have to go to the office.*

B Sino = *but*

When a negative notion is replaced by the positive or corrected equivalent, use **sino** (not **pero**) to translate *but*.

Ésta no es Luisa sino Julia.	*This isn't Luisa but Julia.*
¡No estamos de vacaciones sino de juerga!	*We're not on holiday but on a binge!*
Julia no entra sino sale.	*Julia's not coming in but going out.*

With verb equivalents, **sino que** is often used.

No saludo sino que me ahogo. *I'm not waving but drowning.*

Sino is not used when both elements are negative.

No saludo pero no me ahogo tampoco *I'm not waving but I'm not drowning either.*

C **Sin embargo** = *however*

Estoy en casa; sin embargo   *I'm at home, however I*
no puedo verte.   *can't see you.*

D **No obstante** = *nevertheless*

Pedro es rico; no obstante nunca   *Pedro is rich; nevertheless*
paga la cuenta.   *he never pays the bill.*

exercise

Fill the blanks with *pero* or *sino*.

a Quiero comprar un coche _____ no tengo bastante dinero.

b No quiero comprar un coche _____ una moto.

c No quiero comprar un coche _____ no quiero usar los trenes.

d Voy a salir con Adolfo _____ es un hombre algo feo.

e No voy a salir con Adolfo _____ con Julio.

f No quiero a María _____ ella me quiere mucho.

g María no es española _____ argentina.

h No vive en Madrid _____ Buenos Aires.

i No vive en Madrid _____ su hermana vive allí.

j No es su hermana _____ su hermano que vive allí.

Spanish verbs fall into three basic groups according to their infinitive. This unit covers the regular forms.

A The infinitive is the part of the verb you look up in the dictionary. It corresponds to the English *to speak*, *to eat*, *to live*, etc. In English, *to* is the usual sign of the infinitive, and is a separate word. In Spanish, the infinitive is just one word, and the group is shown by the final two letters: **-ar**, **-er** or **-ir**: hablar *to speak*; comer *to eat*; vivir *to live*.

B In English there are usually only two personal forms in the present tense, for example, *eat*, *eats*. We need to add *I*, *you*, *he*, etc. to show the subject. Spanish, on the other hand, shows the subject by the ending of the verb. There are six forms for each group; three singular and three plural.

		hablar *to speak*	comer *to eat*	vivir *to live*
singular	1	hablo *I...*	como *I...*	vivo *I...*
	2	hablas *you...*	comes *you...*	vives *you...*
	3	habla *he / she / it / you ...*	come *he / she / it / you ...*	vive *he / she / it / you ...*
plural	1	hablamos *we...*	comemos *we...*	vivimos *we...*
	2	habláis *you...*	coméis *you...*	vivís *you...*
	3	hablan *they / you ...*	comen *they / you ...*	viven *they / you...*

C *I* and *we* are known as 'first person', the first people you think about when the ship goes down! *You* (singular and plural) are second persons – the next people on your mind. *He*, *she* and *it* (singular) and *they* (plural) are third persons – those who are left.

D Spanish distinguishes between *you* in the singular (**tú**) and plural (**vosotros**). The second person forms are 'familiar', used when talking to family, friends and people of your age or status.

There are also third-person forms for *you* (**usted** and **ustedes**) which are 'polite' or 'formal' forms – they take third-person verb endings as if to avoid direct address. They are used with strangers, in a formal situation or if you are not sure about status. If in doubt, use these when speaking to someone you don't know.

exercise

Fill the gaps with the verb form from the box.

a Pedro _____ vino.

b _____ en Madrid.

c _____ cartas.

d _____ cigarrillos.

e _____ con mis amigos.

f _____ un libro.

g _____ la catedral.

h _____ patatas.

bebe	charlo	come	escribes	fuman
	lee	visitamos	vivimos	

Many first-person singular forms of the present tense have peculiarities. This unit summarizes some of them.

A First persons in **-go**.

A number of verbs from the **-er** and **-ir** groups insert a **g** before the final **-o** of the first person. This **g** disappears in the other forms of the present tense, which behave normally. An example is **salir** *to go out, leave*:

Salir: salgo, sales, sale, salimos, salís, salen.

Salgo de la casa.   *I go out of the house.*

B Other common verbs with **-g-** in the first person singular include **caer** *to fall* → **caigo, caes, cae**, etc; **poner** *to put* → **pongo, pones, pone**; **traer** *to bring* → **traigo, traes, trae**; **hacer** *to do, make* → **hago, haces, hace**.

Tengo un coche.   *I have a car.*
Digo la verdad.   *I tell the truth.*
Oigo la música.   *I hear the music.*

C **Venir** *to come* behaves like **tener**, but with **-ir** endings: **vengo, vienes, viene, venimos, venís, vienen.**

¿Vienes a la fiesta conmigo? *Are you coming to the party with me?*

D The first person singular of the present tense of most verbs ends in **-o**. However, verbs of one syllable, end in **-oy**.

ser *to be* → soy *I am*   dar *to give* → doy *I give*

E **Ir** *to go* is irregular. Its endings are similar to **dar**. **Estar** *to be* has similar endings.

ir: voy, vas, va, vamos, vais, van.
dar: doy, das, da, damos, dais, dan.
estar: estoy, estás, está, estamos, estáis, están.

F **Saber** *to know* and **ver** *to see* have irregular first person singulars.

saber: sé, sabes, sabe, sabemos, sabéis, saben.
ver: veo, ves, ve, vemos, veis, ven.

G Verbs in **-ecer**, **-ocer** and **-ucir** have **-zco** in their first persons, for example **conocer** *to know, be acquainted*, **ofrecer** *to offer* and **conducir** *to drive*.

conocer: conozco, conoces, conoce, conocemos, conocéis, conocen.
ofrecer: ofrezco, ofreces, ofrece, ofrecemos, ofrecéis, ofrecen.
conducir: conduzco, conduces, conduce, conducimos, conducís, conducen.

Similarly **parecer** *to seem*; **aparecer** *to appear*; **obedecer** *to obey*; **traducir** *to translate*; **producir** *to produce*; **introducir** *to introduce*; **reducir** *to reduce*.

See exercise 20 in 'More practice'.

This unit covers the main spelling changes you have to look out for when giving different forms of the present.

A Changes affecting the first person singular.

- Verbs ending in -ger like **coger** *to pick*; **escoger** *to choose*. The **g** changes to **j** in the first person singular: **cojo** *I pick*; **escojo** *I choose*.

- Verbs ending in -cer like **vencer** *to overcome*; **cocer** *to boil*, **torcer** *to twist*. The **c** changes to **z**: **venzo** *I overcome*; **cuezo** *I boil*; **tuerzo** *I twist*.

- Verbs in -guir like **seguir** *to follow, continue*; **distinguir** *to distinguish* drop the **u** before **o**: **sigo** *I follow*; distingo *I distinguish*.

B Changes affecting other forms of the present.

- Verbs like **continuar** *to continue*; **enviar** *to send*; **prohibir** *to forbid*; **reír** *to laugh* take an accent on the **u** or **i** when this weak vowel is stressed.

		continuar	enviar	prohibir	reír
singular	1 I ...	continúo	envío	prohíbo	río
	2 you ...	continúas	envías	prohíbes	ríes
	3 he/she/it/you...	continúa	envía	prohíbe	ríe
plural	1 we ...	continuamos	enviamos	prohibimos	reímos
	2 you ...	continuáis	enviáis	prohibís	reís
	3 they/you	continúan	envían	prohíben	ríen

Try reciting the verbs out loud to remember the stress.

• Verbs like **oír** *to hear*; **huir** *to flee* insert y in certain forms.

oír: oigo, oyes, oye, oímos, oís, oyen.
huir: huyo, huyes, huye, huimos, huis, huyen.

C Radical-changing verbs (see Unit 44) starting with o- or e- like **oler** *to smell* and **errar** *to wander* put **h** before -ue and change **ie** to **ye**.

oler: huelo, hueles, huele, olemos, oléis, huelen.
errar: yerro, yerras, yerra, erramos, erráis, yerran.

exercise

Put the correct form of the missing verb in the gap.

a Julio siempre _____ en el cine. (**reír**)
b Yo no _____ flores en el parque. (**coger**)
c Juan _____ un regalo para su madre. (**escoger**)
d Yo no _____ Londres. (**conocer**)
e Los ladrones _____ por la calle. (**huir**)
f El niño no _____ a su madre. (**oír**)
g Tú siempre _____ una carta a tu familia. (**enviar**)
h Este vino _____ mal. (**oler**)
i Luisa y Felipe _____ hablando. (**continuar**)
j El policía nos _____ aparcar. (**prohibir**)

Spanish uses two different verbs for *to be*. They are used in different situations.

A These are the present tenses:

		ser	estar	
singuar	1	soy	estoy	*I am*
	2	eres	estás	*you are*
	3	es	está	*he / she / it is, you are*
plural	1	somos	estamos	*we are*
	2	sois	estáis	*you are*
	3	son	están	*they / you are*

You will see that **ser** is irregular. **Estar** behaves like **dar,** but is stressed on the endings throughout – notice the need for accents on most of its forms.

B Fortunately there are some basic rules which cover most uses of these verbs.

• Use **ser** when a noun or pronoun follows as complement.

Soy profesor.	*I'm a teacher.*
Mi madre es enfermera.	*My mother is a nurse.*
Somos estudiantes de inglés.	*We are students of English.*
¿Eres tú, María?	*Is that you, María?*

- The noun may be implied and not actually stated.

Somos (ciudadanos) ingleses.	*We're English.*
Es el (día) dos de mayo.	*It's the second of May.*
Son las tres (horas) de la tarde.	*It's 3 p.m.*
No soy (mujer) española.	*I am not Spanish.*

- **Estar** is used to show position or location.

Madrid está en España.	*Madrid is in Spain*
Juan está en la universidad.	*Juan is at university.*
Estoy aquí en casa.	*I am here at home.*
¿Dónde están los servicios?	*Where are the toilets?*

- Typical uses of **ser** and **estar** can be seen in this telephone conversation.

– ¡Oye! ¿Eres Pedro?	*Hello, is that (you) Pedro?*
– No, soy Juan. Pedro no está.	*No, it's John. Pedro isn't in.*
– Entonces, ¿está su madre?	*Then is his mother there?*

exercise

Put in the correct form of *ser* or *estar* as necessary.

E.g. Emilio y tú _____ estudiantes. → Emilio y tú sois estudiantes.

a María _____ española.

b María _____ en España.

c Los hombres _____ mecánicos.

d Los mecánicos _____ en el garaje.

e ¿Tú _____ en casa?

f ¿Tú _____ Luisa?

Either *ser* or *estar* can be used with adjectives, but they have different implications.

A Ser is used to show inherent characteristics.

Manolo es inteligente.	*Manolo is intelligent.*
Juanita es bonita y delgada.	*Juanita is pretty and slim.*
El hielo es frío.	*Ice is cold.*
América es grande.	*America is big.*
Viajar en avión es rápido.	*Travelling by plane is fast.*
Me gusta este libro – es divertido.	*I like this book – it's funny.*

B Estar is used to show accidental qualities (e.g. what has happened to something or someone).

Julio está triste porque está constipado.	*Julio is sad because he's got a cold.*
Mi café está frío.	*My coffee is cold.*
Esta taza está vacía.	*This cup is empty.*
¡Estás muy alegre esta mañana!	*You seem very cheerful this morning!*
¡Qué constipado estoy!	*How cold-ridden I am!*
¡Qué bonita estás con ese vestido!	*How pretty you look in that dress!*

C Note these changes in meaning.

Julio es aburrido.	*Julio is boring.*
Julio está aburrido.	*Julio is bored.*
Luisa es divertida.	*Luisa is amusing.*
Luisa está divertida.	*Luisa is amused.*

D With a past participle, **ser** shows an action in process (the passive) whereas **estar** describes the state resulting from that action.

La puerta es abierta por el profesor.   *The door is being opened by the teacher.*

Ahora la puerta está abierta.   *Now the door is open.*

E **Estar** is also used to form continuous tenses with the gerund (see Unit 43):

Está abriendo la puerta.   *He is opening the door.*

Estoy escribiendo una carta.   *I'm writing a letter.*

exercise

Complete this letter to a new penfriend by filling the gaps with the correct forms of *ser/estar*.

Yo me llamo Julio y a _____ estudiante y **b** _____ estudiando la historia, que **c** _____ muy difícil pero interesante. Hoy **d** _____ lunes y voy a la universidad pero no **e** _____ bien. Por desgracia **f** _____ muy constipado. Mis amigos también **g** _____ malos y **h** _____ en casa. La universidad **i** _____ en las afueras de la ciudad y **j** _____ muy grande con muchos estudiantes. Ya **k** _____ las nueve y media y hoy **l** _____ la clase del doctor López que **m** _____ un hombre muy antipático y **n** _____ furioso si un estudiante **o** _____ ausente o mal preparado.

The gerund emphasizes actions in progress.

A The gerund in Spanish corresponds to the verb ending in *-ing* in English. It is used when two or more actions take place at the same time.

Iban por la calle, cantando y riendo.	*They were going along the street, singing and laughing.*

B The gerund is formed by replacing the infinitive endings **-ar**, **-er** and **-ir** as follows.

cantar *to sing* → cantando *singing*
comer *to eat* → comiendo *eating*
escribir *to write* → escribiendo *writing*

C Verbs like **leer** *to read* and **creer** *to believe* change the **i** to **y** (leyendo, creyendo).

Continuaron leyendo.	*They went on reading.*

D A small cluster of **-ir** verbs which are radical changing (see Unit 44) have irregular gerunds. These include the following: morir *to die* → muriendo; dormir *to sleep* → durmiendo; pedir *to ask, request* → pidiendo; repetir *to repeat* → repitiendo; seguir *to follow, continue* → siguiendo; reír *to laugh* → riendo; decir *to say* → diciendo.

E The gerund is used after **estar** *to be* (see Unit 41) to form 'progressive' tenses, which emphasize an action actually taking place.

| Niños, vuestra madre está hablando. | *Children, your mother is speaking.* |
| Mira, el tren está saliendo. | *Look, the train is leaving.* |

Estar can be used in any appropriate tense.

| Los pájaros estaban cantando y volando por el cielo. | *The birds were singing and flying across the sky.* |

Use the infinitive and not the gerund in expressions such as the following.

| Me gusta leer. | *I like reading.* |
| Ver es creer. | *Seeing is believing.* |

F The gerund is used after two verbs, **continuar** and **seguir**, to mean *to continue, to go on …ing.*

| Julio continuó hablando. | *Julio kept on talking.* |

exercise

Change the ordinary present into the continuous present.

E.g. hablamos → estamos hablando.

a estudiamos

b reímos

c muere

d roban

e aprendo

f salís

g escribes

h espera

i seguimos

j repiten

In some verbs, the root vowel changes when the stress falls on it. Such verbs are usually known as 'radical-changing', 'root-changing' or 'stem-changing verbs'.

Radical-changing verbs can come from any of the three groups (-ar, -er or -ir). The change doesn't affect the first and second persons plural (**nosotros** and **vosotros**) because the stress doesn't fall on the root vowel.

A Root o → ue

contar *to count, relate*	poder *to be able/can*	dormir *to sleep*
cuento	puedo	duermo
cuentas	puedes	duermes
cuenta	puede	duerme
contamos	podemos	dormimos
contáis	podéis	dormís
cuentan	pueden	duermen

B Root e → ie

pensar *to think*	querer *to want*	sentir *to feel*
pienso	quiero	siento
piensas	quieres	sientes
piensa	quiere	siente
pensamos	queremos	sentimos
pensáis	queréis	sentís
piensan	quieren	sienten

C Some common verbs like **tener** *to have* and **venir** *to come* do not have a radical change in the first person if they have already inserted -**g**-; the rest of the verb, however, follows the above pattern.

tener: tengo, tienes, tiene, tenemos, tenéis, tienen.

venir: vengo, vienes, viene, venimos, venís, vienen.

There are also a few verbs in the -**ir** group that change the root **e** to **i**.

pedir *to request*: pido, pides, pide, pedimos, pedís, piden.

Some common verbs like this are: **seguir** *to follow, continue*; **repetir** *to repeat*; **servir** *to serve*; **reír** *to laugh*; **sonreír** *to smile*.

exercise

Put the verb in the correct form to tell the story.

Todos los días, cuando yo me (**a** vestir), Julia me (**b** servir) el café que (**c** hervir) en la cocina. Yo (**d** pensar) que Julia y los hijos (**e** tener) mucho más que hacer en la casa pero Julia me (**f** sonreír) mientras (**g** seguir) trabajando. A las diez, los vecinos (**h** venir) y siempre (**i** repetir) las noticias del día. (**j** Decir) que (**k** querer) una taza de café también y nos (**l** contar) todos sus chistes. Julia y yo (**m** reír) mucho y los vecinos (**n** reír) también. Sus chistes nos (**o** divertir) siempre. Pero, después de media hora yo no (**p** poder) más – (**q** perder) mucho tiempo. Yo (**r** sonreír), y (**s** pedir) perdón y (**t** volver) a mi trabajo. Por la tarde me (**u** sentir) un poco cansado, y (**v** dormir) la siesta – Julia (**w** dormir) también porque (**x** tener) sueño.

Relexive verbs are very common in Spanish and frequently translate the idea of a person or thing becoming or getting something.

A Reflexive verbs are used with a reflexive pronoun agreeing with (or 'reflecting') the subject. The reflexive pronoun is attached to the end of the infinitive: **lavarse** *to get washed*. When the verbs have a personal ending, the reflexive pronoun goes in front of the verb.

lavarse *to get washed*	ponerse *to put on*	vestirse *to get dressed*
me lavo	me pongo	me visto
te lavas	te pones	te vistes
se lava	se pone	se viste
nos lavamos	nos ponemos	nos vestimos
os laváis	os ponéis	os vestís
se lavan	se ponen	se visten

Remember that **usted** and **ustedes** are treated as third persons so they take the reflexive pronoun **se**.

Compare these verbs used reflexively and non-reflexively.

Lavo los platos.	*I wash the dishes.*
Me lavo en el cuarto de baño.	*I get washed in the bathroom.*
Acostamos al bebé.	*We put the baby to bed.*
Nos acostamos.	*We go to bed.*

Other verbs like this include **levantarse** *to get up*; **bañarse** *to have a bath / go bathing*; **ducharse** *to have a shower*; **maquillarse** *to put on make-up*; **desnudarse** *to get undressed*; **quitarse** *to take off (clothing)*; **dormirse** *to fall asleep*; **divertirse** *to have a good time*.

Me pongo el pijama.	*I put on my pyjamas.*
Se visten rápidamente.	*They get dressed quickly.*
Los niños se divierten mucho en el circo.	*The children have a good time / enjoy themselves at the circus.*

C Note the word order if subject pronouns are used for emphasis, or the verb is negative.

Yo me lavo pero tú no te lavas. *I get washed but you don't.*

exercise

Say what you do at the following times.

Spanish also has several reflexive verbs which indicate or emphasize types of movement or change of position.

A Several verbs suggest movement away when they are reflexive. An example is **ir** *to go* and **irse** *to go away*.

irse: me voy, te vas, se va, nos vamos, os vais, se van.

¡Me voy!	*I'm off!*
Los niños se van por la calle.	*The children go off down the street.*

Like **irse** are **marcharse** *to go away*; **escaparse** *to escape*; **correrse** *to run away*.

Si no pagas, me marcho.	*If you don't pay, I'm leaving.*

B A reflexive verb is sometimes used for emphasis: **caer** *to fall*; **caerse** *to fall down, over*.

¡Cuidado! ¡Vas a caerte!	*Careful – you'll fall over!*

C Other verbs involving movement are reflexive, especially if an object is not stated: **detenerse, pararse** *to stop*; **moverse** *to move*; **perderse** *to get lost*; **pasearse** *to go for a stroll, walk*.

El autobús se para por enfrente.	*The bus stops opposite.*
Estoy cansado – no puedo moverme.	*I'm tired – I can't move.*

NB El chófer para el coche.   *The driver stops the car.*

C There are two ways to combine reflexive verbs with other verbs; you can use either word order.

Voy a divertirme. / Me voy a   *I'm going to have a good time.*
divertir.

NB Never put the reflexive pronoun between the two verbs.

exercise

Give the correct form of the verb in brackets.

E.g. El tren (pararse) en la estación. → El tren se para en la estación.

a El coche (pararse) en el garaje.

b La policía (parar) los coches.

c Yo siempre (perder) dinero.

d Yo siempre (perderse) en Madrid.

e El niño (caerse) mucho en la playa.

f Las hojas (caer) en octubre.

g La policía (detener) a los ladrones.

h Luisa (detenerse) para ver el tráfico.

i ¿Quiere usted (mover) su coche? No puedo salir.

j Julio no va a (moverse) porque está cansado.

This unit looks at ways of making general statements.

A Like English, Spanish usually refers to a specific subject.

Juan bebe vino.	*Juan drinks wine.*
Los españoles hablan español.	*Spaniards speak Spanish.*

Sometimes, however, you want to make a general statement.

En España beben mucho vino.	*In Spain they drink a lot of wine.*

In this sentence, *they* means 'people in general'. Spanish, like English, can simply use the third person plural (the *they* form) of the verb.

Dicen que va a llover.	*They say it's going to rain.*

Spanish also uses the reflexive **se** with a singular verb.

Se dice que va a llover.	*It is said it's going to rain.*
Aquí se habla español.	*They speak Spanish here. / Spanish is spoken here.*

This construction is very common when the verb does not take a direct object, and corresponds to the English *one*.

Aquí se vive bien.	*You / People live / One lives well here.*
Se estudia mucho.	*You / People study / One studies hard.*

B **Se puede** is a useful expression to ask if something is permitted.

¿Se puede aparcar aquí?   *Can one park here?*
¿Se puede pagar con tarjeta   *Can you pay by credit card?*
  de crédito?

C With a reflexive verb which already has a **se**, **uno** is used as the subject.

En el campo uno se levanta   *In the countryside people get up*
  temprano.   *early / one gets up early.*
Uno se divierte mucho en   *You have / One has a good*
  la fiesta.   *time at the party.*

You can also use **la gente** *people*, again with a singular verb.

La gente se divierte mucho en   *People have a good time at*
  la fiesta.   *the party.*
En España la gente es simpática.   *In Spain, people are kind.*

exercise

Use *se puede* to ask if something is allowed.

E.g. Quiero aparcar. → ¿Se puede aparcar aquí?

a Quiero pagar con dinero inglés.
b Quiero telefonear.
c Quiero comprar sellos.
d Quiero sacar fotos.
e Quiero cambiar dinero.
f Quiero usar una tarjeta de crédito.
g Quiero nadar.
h Quiero visitar la catedral.

To express the idea of liking, Spanish uses the verb *gustar* – literally *to be pleasing*.

A Gustar is used 'back-to-front', with the indirect object pronoun to show who is doing the liking (or disliking); it is used in the third person singular (**gusta**) if one thing is liked, or in the third person plural (**gustan**) if more than one thing is liked. In other words, the thing(s) being liked are the *subject* of the verb.

(no)	me gusta	(no)	me gustan
	te gusta		te gustan
	le gusta		le gustan
	nos gusta		nos gustan
	os gusta		os gustan
	les gusta		les gustan

| Les gusta el vino. | *They like the wine* (lit. *to them is pleasing the wine.*) |
| Les gustan las patatas. | *They like the potatoes* (lit. *to them are pleasing the potatoes*). |

B The definite article is used to show general likes or dislikes.
Me gusta el queso. *I like cheese.*

C The singular **gusta** is used with a verb.
Me gusta bailar y cantar. *I like singing and dancing.*

D If a name or a particular person or persons are referred to, they are introduced with **a**.

A Juan le gusta el cine.	*John likes cinema.*
A Julia no le gustan las naranjas.	*Julia doesn't like oranges.*
Al profesor le gusta cantar.	*The teacher likes singing.*
A las chicas les gusta esta tienda.	*Girls like this shop.*

E The personal indirect object pronouns can be intensified for clarity or emphasis by adding the disjunctive pronouns (see Unit 27) with **a**.

A mí me gusta bailar, pero a ti no te gusta.	*I like dancing, but you don't.*

You can only use one personal pronoun in front of **gustar**.

NB Since **gustar** means *to be pleasing*, any other personal verb ending needs care.

Me gustas.	*I fancy you* (lit. *you are pleasing to me*).

exercise

Say whether the person likes or dislikes something.

E.g. Juan ☺ cantar → A Juan le gusta cantar.

a María ☹ el vino blanco.
b Julio y Julia ☺ el teatro.
c yo ☹ trabajar.
d Julia ☺ salir con Julio.
e tú ☺ ¿la paella?
f tu y yo ☹ las novelas.

Besides *gustar*, Spanish has a number of expressions using verbs with indirect object pronouns.

A Doler (*to be aching, be hurting*)

Me duele la cabeza.	*I have a headache* (lit. *to me is aching the head*).
Me duelen los pies.	*I have sore feet* (lit. *to me are aching the feet*).

Me *to me* is an indirect pronoun. It indicates the person being affected. The indirect object pronoun is kept even when a specific person is mentioned.

A Julio le duelen las piernas.	*Julio's legs are aching.*

If, however, you want to say that someone is hurting you, say:

Me haces daño.	*You're hurting me.*
El dentista siempre me hace daño.	*The dentist always hurts me.*

B There are other more pleasant verbs that follow the same pattern: **encantar** *to delight*; **chiflar** *to captivate, drive crazy*; **apetecer** *to appeal to*.

Me encanta el vino.	*I love the wine.*
A Julia le encantan las gambas.	*Julia loves prawns.*
Me chifla el fútbol.	*I'm mad about football.*
No me apetece salir esta noche.	*I don't feel like going out tonight.*

C Other common expressions of this type include:

- **(me, etc.) hace falta** *I need*
  Me hace falta descansar. *I need to rest.*
  Le hacen falta unos buenos *He could do with some*
  amigos. *good friends.*
- **me falta** *I'm short of* (lit. *to me is lacking*)
- **me importa** *it matters to me*
  Francamente, cariño, no me *Frankly, my dear, I don't*
  importa un pepino. *give a damn!* (lit. *it doesn't*
  matter a cucumber to
  me!)
- **me queda** *I have … left*
  Me quedan sólo diez libras. *I've only ten pounds left.*
- **me conviene** *it suits me*
- **me sienta** *it suits / looks good on me*
  Te sienta bien ese vestido. *That dress suits you.*
- **a mí me toca** *it's my turn*

Practise this one, just in case:
  ¡Me ha tocado el gordo! *I've won the lottery!*

See exercise 24 in 'More practice'.

Impersonal expressions are statements like *it is difficult to sleep; it is forbidden to smoke*.

A If the expression refers to a general situation, i.e. no particular person is included, you may follow with the verb in the infinitive.

Es difícil estudiar.	*It's difficult to study.*
No es posible ir en autobús.	*You / One can't go by bus.*
Hace falta ir a pie.	*You / One must go on foot.*
Es mejor usar el ascensor.	*It's better to use the lift.*
Está prohibido aparcar.	*It's forbidden to park.*

B To relate the expression to a particular person, use an indirect object.

Me es difícil trabajar.	*I find it hard to work.*
Te es imposible llegar a tiempo.	*You can't get there on time.*
Nos hace falta esperar aquí.	*We have to wait here.*

C When the speaker is expressing a personal opinion or making a value judgement about something or someone else, a subjunctive verb is needed.

Hay mucha niebla y es imposible que venga.	*It's very foggy and it's impossible for him to get here.*
Lo más importante es que usted trabaje mucho.	*The most important thing is that you work hard.*
Es curioso que David no hable bien el español.	*It's strange that David does not speak Spanish well.*

The subjunctive verb may have to be in a past tense.

Sería importante que Julio viniera a tiempo.
It would be important for Julio to come on time.

Habría sido inútil que los bomberos entrasen en el edificio.
It would have been useful for the firemen to go into the building.

D Hay que + infinitive is also used to make a general statement:

Hay que trabajar mucho.
One must work hard.

Había que comer poco.
It was necessary to eat little.

exercise

Answer each question with an appropriate infinitive expression.

E.g. ¿Dónde cojo el autobús? (imposible) → Es imposible coger un autobús.

a ¿Dónde alquilo un coche? (difícil)

b ¿Se puede aparcar aquí? (está prohibido)

c Estoy muy cansado. ¿Qué recomienda usted – ir en taxi o a pie? (es más rápido)

d La reparación es urgente. ¿Debo ir al taller? (más vale)

e ¿Se recomienda comer temprano? (preferible)

We use the preterite or simple past tense to indicate completed actions carried out in the past.

A These are the regular forms of the preterite.

hablar *to speak*	comer *to eat*	escribir *to write*
hablé	comí	escribí
hablaste	comiste	escribiste
habló	comió	escribió
hablamos	comimos	escribimos
hablasteis	comisteis	escribisteis
hablaron	comieron	escribieron

B Note the following

- -er and -ir verbs share the same set of endings.
- The **nosotros** *we* form is the same as in the present tense for -ar and -ir verbs, but different for -er verbs.
- Stressed -ó or -ió is the third person singular form in the preterite (not to be confused with the first-person -o ending in the present tense).

Ayer visité a mi amigo en Londres.

Yesterday I visited my friend in London.

Julio cogió el bocadillo y se lo comió en seguida.

Julio picked up the sandwich and ate it straight away.

Viví seis años en París.

I lived for six years in Paris.

- Sometimes the spelling will have to change.

  empezar *to begin*: empecé, empezaste, etc.

  llegar *to arrive*: llegué, llegaste, etc.

- Accent marks are not needed for verbs of one syllable such as **ver** *to see*, **dar** *to give*.

  ver: vi, viste, vio, vimos, visteis, vieron.

- **Dar** has -er/-ir endings in the preterite, like **ver**:

  dar: di, diste, dio, dimos, disteis, dieron.

Ayer vi la televisión.	*Yesterday I watched television.*
Mi amigo me dio un regalo.	*My friend gave me a present.*

C Time expressions

ayer *yesterday*; anoche *last night*; anteayer *the day before yesterday*, el año / lunes pasado *last year / Monday* etc.; hace cinco años *five years ago* etc.

exercise

Give the preterite for the following verbs.

E.g. tú (hablar) → tú hablaste

a él (saltar = *to jump*)

b nosotros (abrir = *to open*)

c ustedes (correr = *to run*)

d yo (cerrar = *to close*)

e vosotros (escuchar = *to listen*)

f nosotros (sentarse = *to sit down*)

g ellos (volver = *to return*)

h tú (sentir = *to feel*)

i ellos (contestar = *to reply*)

A very few verbs have stem changes in the preterite. You will have already met some of these verbs in the present tense.

A The good news is that no verbs in -ar or -er have radical changes in the preterite. However, a cluster of verbs from the -ir group do change their stem in the third-person forms of the preterite.

B The first type changes e to i:

pedir *to ask for, request*: pedí, pediste, pidió, pedimos, pedisteis, pidieron

Other verbs like **pedir** are **seguir** *to follow, continue*; **sentir** (*to feel*; **repetir** *to repeat*; **servir** *to serve*; **hervir** *to boil*; **divertirse** *to have a good time*; **arrepentirse** *to repent, regret*.

Juan me pidió dinero.	*Juan asked me for money.*
Los camareros sirvieron la comida.	*The waiters served the meal.*
Julio se divirtió mucho.	*Julio had a very good time.*

C The second type changes o to u:

dormir *to sleep*: dormí, dormiste, durmió, dormimos, dormisteis, durmieron

Morir *to die* changes in the same way.

Anoche durmieron bien.	*Last night they slept well.*
El general Franco murió en 1975.	*General Franco died in 1975.*

NB Only the third persons change, and these verbs have similar changes in the gerund.

D The irregular verbs **ir** *to go* and **ser** *to be* share the same forms in the preterite: **fui, fuiste, fue, fuimos, fuisteis, fueron.**

Ayer fui a Londres a visitar a mi amigo.	*Yesterday I went to London to visit my friend.*
Julio fue al cine con sus amigos.	*Julio went to the cinema with his friends.*
Pedro y Juan fueron buenos amigos.	*Pedro and Juan were good friends.*
Los ladrones fueron cogidos por la policía.	*The robbers were caught by the police.*
La reunión fue abierta por el presidente.	*The meeting was opened by the president.*

Don't confuse **fui** *I went, I was* and **fue** *he went, he was.* **Ir** and **ser** are the only preterites that end in **-e** in the third person singular!

exercise

Fill the gaps in the story using *pedir, servir, repetir* and *seguir*.

Ayer, en un bar yo **a** _____ una cerveza. El camarero me **b** _____ vino.

– No, cerveza, **c** _____ .

– ¿Cerveza? **d** _____ el camerero.

– Sí, cerveza, yo **e** _____ .

– No, usted me **f** _____ vino, **g** _____ repitiendo el camerero.

Pero por fin el camarero me **h** _____ la cerveza que **i** _____ .

A group of verbs forms the preterite in a slightly different way, known as the *pretérito grave*.

A The pretérito grave endings are: -e, -iste, -o, -imos, -isteis, -ieron.

estar *to be*	poner *to put*	venir *to come*
estuve	puse	vine
estuviste	pusiste	viniste
estuvo	puso	vino
estuvimos	pusimos	vinimos
estuvisteis	pusisteis	vinisteis
estuvieron	pusieron	vinieron

Mis padres vinieron a verme. *My parents came to see me.*
Me puse el mejor traje.   *I put on my best suit.*

B Unlike the so-called regular preterites, **pretérito grave** verbs are not stressed on the end. Never put an accent mark on them. To add to the fun, the stem of the verb usually changes in a somewhat unpredictable way.

All verbs of this sort, whether **-ar**, **-er** or **-ir**, share the same set of endings.

C Other common verbs in this cluster are:
poder *to be able*: pude, pudiste, …
andar *to walk, function (machinery)*: anduve, anduviste, …
saber *to know*: supe, supiste, …

querer *to want, love*: quise, quisiste, ...
tener *to have*: tuve, tuviste, ...
hacer *to do, make*: hice, hiciste, ...

Julio no pudo abrir la puerta.	*Julio was not able to open the door.*
Las chicas hicieron una empanada.	*The girls made a pie.*

D Remember the spelling rules concerning c/z (Unit 1) with **hacer** (*to do, make*): the c changes to a z in the third person singular (**hizo**).

Hizo sus deberes anoche.	*He did his homework last night.*

E Verbs ending in -ucir like **conducir** *to drive* all change the ending to -**uje**: conducir → conduje; producir *to produce* → produje

F One more thing to remember: after a -j- you write -**eron** instead of -**ieron**: decir *to say*: dije, dijiste, dijo, dijimos, dijisteis, dijeron

Por fin dijeron la verdad.	*At last they told the truth.*

See exercise 26 in 'More practice'.

The imperfect tense is used to describe actions in the past which were repeated, in process or not necessarily completed.

A There is usually no specific reference to the action's start or end, hence the name 'imperfect'. Examples in English are: *I used to go, I was going, I would go*. It is used with expressions like **todos los días** *every day*, **con frecuencia** *frequently*, **muchas veces / a menudo** *often*. Spanish has only two sets of endings. The stress stays on the same syllable throughout.

B Only two verbs – **ser** *to be* and **ir** *to go* – have strange imperfects. **Ver** *to see* reflects its old infinitive form, **veer**, by inserting an extra **e** before the endings.

Veían la televisión en vez de estudiar.	*They would watch television instead of studying.*
Iba a la corrida, pero ya no.	*I used to go to the bullfight, but no longer.*

hablar	comer	vivir
hablaba	comía	vivía
hablabas	comías	vivías
hablaba	comía	vivía
hablábamos	comíamos	vivíamos
hablabais	comíais	vivíais
hablaban	comían	vivían

ser	ir	ver
era	iba	veía
eras	ibas	veías
era	iba	veía
éramos	íbamos	veíamos
erais	ibais	veíais
eran	iban	veían

Note the need for an accent on **hablábamos**, and the -í- throughout the -er and -ir verbs.

Todos los días hablábamos italiano.	*We would speak Italian every day.*
Vivían entonces en Nerja.	*They were living in Nerja at that time.*
Te llamaba – ¿dónde estabas?	*I was calling you – where were you?*

As the first and third persons singular are identical, a subject pronoun may be required for clarity.

Antes (yo) nunca comía carne.	*I never used to eat meat.*

C Spanish can also emphasize habit or custom by using **soler** *to be in the habit of* with an infinitive.

Solíamos ir de vacaciones a España.	*We normally went to Spain for our holidays.*

exercise

Say what you no longer do.

E.g. fumar (yo) → **Fumaba antes, pero ya no.**

a Cantar (yo)

b ser estudiantes (nosotros)

c nadar (Luisa)

d practicar deportes (tú)

e ir de paseo (yo)

f escribir (Julio e Isabel)

g estudiar (tú y yo)

h ver los partidos (ustedes)

i ayudar (vosotros)

j leer mucho (yo)

Choosing whether to use imperfect or preterite when talking about the past is normally fairly straightforward.

A The preterite is used for a specific, completed action.

El año pasado Julio ganó la lotería.	*Last year Julio won the lottery.*

B The imperfect is used for repeated or general actions.

Cuando era niño estudiaba mucho.	*When I was a child I would study a lot.*

C Usually an English verb such as *used to (study)*, *was (studying)*, *would (study)* is a clear indication for the imperfect, whereas *went*, *visited*, *won* suggest a preterite. Care is sometimes needed, however.

Cuando éramos niños fuimos a Madrid.	*When we were children we went to Madrid.*

(**fuimos** = preterite, one occasion implied)

Cuando éramos niños íbamos a Madrid todos los veranos.	*When we were children we went to Madrid every summer.*

(**íbamos** = imperfect, as the action was repeated)

D The preterite is used with actions that imply a beginning or end when a time duration is stated – even if that time period is a long one.

Vivimos allí cuarenta años.	*We lived there for forty years.*

The imperfect is used for setting the scene or explaining the situation. The preterite is used for a specific event.

| Mientras tomábamos café en la terraza, empezó a llover. | *While we were having coffee on the terrace, it started to rain.* |

E With certain verbs, a change of tense from imperfect to preterite can have a different emphasis or meaning.

| Sabía el precio. | *I knew the price.* |
| Supe el precio. | *I found out the price.* |

| Conocía a Julio en Madrid. | *I knew Julio in Madrid.* |
| Conocí a Julio en Madrid. | *I met Julio in Madrid.* |

| No querían venir. | *They did not want to come.* |
| No quisieron venir. | *They refused to come.* |

F Only the imperfect is used to tell the time in the past.

| ¿Qué hora era? | *What time was it?* |
| Eran las cinco y media. | *It was half past five.* |

exercise

What was the weather like when …?

E.g. Ignacio/salir - hacer sol → Hacía sol cuando Ignacio salió.

a Luisa/comprar la fruta/hacer frío
b Mi madre/ir a la ciudad/el sol brilla
c Nosotros/entrar/llover
d Mi padre/ir a trabajar/nevar
e Yo/salir a nadar/hacer viento
f Los estudiantes/comenzar a estudiar/hacer sol

Spanish has many ways to describe an action in the future. This is one of them.

A The future tense is formed by adding personal endings (originally from **haber** *to have*) to the infinitive. The good news is that all verbs (**-ar**, **-er**, **-ir**) share the same set of endings.

hablar	comer	vivir
hablaré	comeré	viviré
hablarás	comerás	vivirás
hablará	comerá	vivirá
hablaremos	comeremos	viviremos
hablaréis	comeréis	viviréis
hablarán	comerán	vivirán

All the endings are stressed, so remember the need for accent marks on all the endings except for **nosotros**.

B The future tense corresponds to the English verb with *shall* or *will* (or simply *'ll*) and explains what will happen at some future time.

Mañana hablaremos más.	*Tomorrow we shall speak again.*
¿Comerás paella en España?	*Will you eat paella in Spain?*
La próxima vez escribirá una carta.	*Next time he'll write a letter.*

C Although the endings are always the same, a few verbs are shortened before adding the endings. This is usually to make the words easier to say.

querer *to want, love*: querré, querrás, …
poder *to be able*: podré, podrás, …
saber *to know*: sabré, sabrás, …
decir *to say*: diré, dirás, …
hacer *to do, make*: haré, harás, …

D Another group inserts **-d-** before the ending.

poner *to put*: pondré, pondrás, pondrá, …
salir *to go out, leave*: saldré, saldrás, …
tener *to have*: tendré, tendrás, …
venir *to come*: vendré, vendrás, …
valer *to be worth*: valdré, valdrás, …

Después de las vacaciones tendremos que trabajar.	*After the holidays we shall have to work.*
Un día esta casa valdrá mucho dinero.	*One day this house will be worth a lot of money.*

See exercise 29 in 'More practice'.

Spanish has a variety of ways to talk about the future. This unit summarizes the main expressions.

A To express actions in the future, Spanish can use the future tense (see Unit 56).

Nos visitará todos los años.	*He will visit us every year.*
Un día iremos a América.	*One day we'll go to America.*

B Particularly in conversation, the ordinary present tense is used when it is clear that the immediate future is intended.

Lo hago ahora mismo.	*I'll do it right now.*
Te llamo mañana.	*I'll call you tomorrow.*

The present is also common with information or instructions.

¿Sirvo el café?	*Shall I serve the coffee?*
¿Doblamos aquí?	*Shall we turn here?*
Dame el dinero o tiro.	*Give me the money or I'll shoot.*

C As in English, **ir a** *to be going to* with the infinitive is very common.

Esta tarde vamos a descansar.	*We're going to rest this afternoon.*
Si no te doy el dinero, ¿qué vas a hacer?	*If I don't give you the money, what will you do?*

D You can use the verb **pensar** with the infinitive to mean *to intend.*

Después de los estudios pensamos casarnos.	*After our studies we intend to get married.*

| Juanito, ¿no piensas lavar los platos? | *Juanito, aren't you going to wash the dishes?* |

E You can also use the verb **querer** *to want* with the infinitive.

| Luisa quiere trabajar mañana. | *Luisa wants to work tomorrow.* |
| No queremos hacerlo. | *We won't do it.* |

exercise

Contrast the future tense with *ir a* + infinitive.

E.g. hablaremos → vamos a hablar

a Comeremos mucho.

b Juan beberá una cerveza.

c Luisa irá a la universidad.

d Tú visitarás América.

e Tendrás problemas.

Use *pensar* + the infinitive to reply to the questions.

E.g. ¿Irás a la universidad? → Sí, pienso ir a la universidad.

f ¿Lavarás los platos?

g ¿Saldrás con Julio?

h ¿Juan comerá toda la paella?

i ¿Usted pagará la cuenta?

j ¿Servirás la comida?

The conditional tense is used to say what would happen in certain circumstances.

A This tense corresponds to the English *should* or *would* when talking about some theoretical possibility.

En ese caso hablaría con el médico.	*In that case I should speak to the doctor.*

B The conditional tense is also used to report 'the future-in-the-past'.

Juan dijo que compraría un coche.	*Juan said that he would buy a car.*

C The conditional tense is formed by adding endings (originally from the imperfect of **haber** *to have*) to the infinitive, in the same way that the future tense (see Unit 56) added endings derived from the present tense of **haber**. As with the future, all verbs share the same sets of endings.

hablar	comer	vivir
hablaría	comería	viviría
hablarías	comerías	vivirías
hablaría	comería	viviría
hablaríamos	comeríamos	viviríamos
hablaríais	comeríais	viviríais
hablarían	comerían	vivirían

The endings are stressed on the same letter throughout, and all endings need **í**.

A mí no me gustaría comer
calamares.
I wouldn't like to eat squid.

D The same infinitives which change to form the future change in the same way to form their conditional: querer → querría, etc.; poner → pondría, etc.

Sin tu ayuda no tendríamos
nada.
*Without your help we would
have nothing.*

exercise

Julio does something but his twin Pedro uses the conditional to say that he wouldn't.

Bebo mucho.   No bebería mucho.

a Como calamares.
b Voy a pie.
c Veo la televisión.
d Salgo con Luisa.
e Hablo con el médico.

f Trabajo mucho.
g Digo la verdad.
h Escribo una carta.
i Puedo llegar a tiempo.
j Sé la dirección.

The present perfect tense is one of many tenses that use *have* to express completed or perfected actions.

A The present perfect (sometimes called just the perfect) is used, as in English, to talk about recent time.

Hemos hablado con tu profesor.	*We have spoken to your teacher.*

B Spanish forms such tenses in the same way, using a form of the verb **haber** *to have* next to a past participle (e.g. *spoken*). Note that **haber** not **tener** is used. This is its irregular present tense: haber *to have*: he, has, ha, hemos, habéis, han.

C The past participle is, fortunately, more regular.

hablar	comer	vivir
hablado	comido	vivido

Once again, -er and -ir verbs follow the same pattern. Verbs like **leer** *to read*, **creer** *to believe* need an accent: **leído, creído**.

D As in English, the past participle does not change.

Has comido mucho.	*You have eaten a lot.*
Hemos vivido en España.	*We have lived in Spain.*

E To make the verb negative, put **no** in front of **haber**. Do not split up **haber**, the past participle and any object or reflexive pronouns.

Tú no te has levantado todavía. *You haven't got up yet.*

F Some past participles (not from -ar verbs) are irregular.

- decir *to say* → dicho; hacer *to do, make* → hecho; escribir *to write* → escrito; poner *to put* → puesto; ver *to see* → visto; romper *to break* → roto; morir *to die* → muerto; freír *to fry* → frito

- Verbs ending in -**brir** have past participles ending in -**bierto**. abrir *to open* → abierto; cubrir *to cover* → cubierto

- Verbs ending in -**olver** have past participles ending in -**uelto**. volver *to return* → vuelto; resolver *to resolve* → resuelto

- Compounds such as **describir, imponer, devolver** are similarly irregular: describir *to describe* → descrito; imponer *to impose* → impuesto; devolver *to give back* → devuelto

exercise

Give the correct form of the present perfect.

E.g. We have spoken (hablar) → Hemos hablado.

a They have eaten (**comer**).

b Have you (**tú**) finished (**terminar**)?

c They have believed (**creer**).

d He has seen (**ver**).

e We have put (**poner**).

f He has died (**morir**).

g You (**vosotros**) have broken (**romper**).

h I have described (**describir**).

i They have returned (**volver**).

j You (**usted**) have written (**escribir**).

This compound tense with *haber* anticipates completed actions in the future.

A The future perfect describes an action or event that will have taken place at some time in the future; the tense is similarly formed in Spanish and English.

Lo habrán terminado pronto.   *They will have finished it soon.*

B The future perfect is formed from the future tense of **haber** *to have* and the past participle.

haber: habré, habrás, habrá, habremos, habréis, habrán

Habré hablado con el médico.	*I shall have spoken to the doctor.*
Habremos comido todo.	*We will have eaten everything.*
Habrán salido.	*They will have gone out.*

Remember the irregular past participles (see Unit 59).

Lo habrás escrito.	*You will have written it.*
Habrán hecho la paella.	*They will have made the paella.*

C The future perfect can also suggest probability, as in English.

Es tarde, el tren habrá salido ya.	*It's late, the train will have left already.*
Habrá muerto.	*He will have died.*

D Some useful expressions which may be used with the future perfect include: pronto *soon*; para finales de la semana *by the end of the week*; para las tres *by three o' clock*; para entonces *by then*; antes de + infinitive *before*.

Lo habré leído antes de salir. *I shall have read it before I go out.*

Remember the word order as with other compound tenses: subject + **no** + object/reflexive pronoun + **haber** + past participle.

Tú no te habrás acostado. *You won't have gone to bed.*
Ellos no se habrán casado. *They won't have got married.*

exercise

Build sentences with the future perfect using the suggestions below.

E.g. Luisa/llegar/a Madrid → Luisa habrá llegado a Madrid.

a Pedro/terminar/su libro
b Yo/pintar/la casa
c Julia y Emilio/casarse
d Tú y Julio/freír/el pescado
e El pobre hombre/morir

f Tú y yo/recibir/el dinero
g Usted/hacer/una paella
h Tú/escribir/la carta
i Ellos/irse/del pueblo
j Ustedes/ver/la película

The past perfect is another 'compound tense' formed with *haber* (to have) and a past participle.

A The past perfect (or 'pluperfect') tense corresponds to the English *had* with the past participle, for example, *I had spoken*, *we had eaten*.

Spanish uses the imperfect tense (see Unit 54) of **haber** *to have*, with the corresponding past participle.

haber: había, habías, había, habíamos, habíais, habían

NB Remember not to use **tener** *to have* to form tenses.

B The past participles are the same regular and irregular ones you met with the present perfect tense (Unit 59).

habíamos hablado	*we had spoken*
había vivido	*he / she had lived*
habías visto	*you had seen*
habían escrito	*they had written*

C As its name implies, the past perfect is used to describe a completed action in the past that happened before something else.

Como había recibido la carta, Juan sabía la verdad.	*As he had received the letter, Juan knew the truth.*
Julio no hablaba portugués porque nunca lo había estudiado.	*Julio didn't speak Portuguese because he had never studied it.*
Yo me había levantado ya cuando mis amigos llegaron.	*I had already got up when my friends arrived.*

Cuando Isabel llegó a casa, los ladrones ya se habían escapado.

When Isabel got home, the robbers had already escaped.

D As with the present perfect (and other tenses formed with **haber**), do not split up the two parts of the verb. In negatives, the **no** comes in front of any object or reflexive pronouns but after any subject pronouns.

Nosotros no la habíamos visto. *We had not seen her.*

exercise

Make as many sentences as possible by joining expressions from A, B, C, D and E.

A	B	C	D	E
Cuando	yo	había	terminado	salimos juntos.
Como	Carlos y María	habíamos	llegado	me acosté.
Tan pronto como *(as soon as)*	nosotros	habías	llamado	tomamos un café.
	tú	habían	salido	vi la televisión.
	la policía			explicamos el problema.

This compound tense with *haber* describes an action or event in the past that would have happened in certain circumstances.

A The conditional perfect is formed as in English, using the conditional tense of **haber** *to have* plus the past participle.

Habría hablado.   *He would have spoken.*

haber: habría, habrías, habría, habríamos, habríais, habrían

B These are followed by the past participles we have already met in Unit 59.

Habríamos hablado español.	*We would have spoken Spanish.*
Julio habría comprado un coche.	*Julio would have bought a car.*
Habrías comido demasiado.	*You would have eaten too much.*
Probablemente Luisa habría salido contigo.	*Luisa would probably have gone out with you.*
En tu sitio habría dicho la verdad.	*In your place I would have told the truth.*
En ese caso habríamos llamado a la policía.	*In that case we would have called the police.*
Con mejor tiempo, Luisa se habría bañado en el mar.	*In better weather, Luisa would have bathed in the sea.*

C The conditional perfect can express probability or supposition about the past.

El rey habría muerto.   *The king would have died.*

A las ocho habría salido ya.   *At eight o'clock he would*
                                 have already left.

D The word order, as with the other compound tenses with
haber, is subject + **no** + object/reflexive pronoun + **haber** +
past participle.

Viviendo en el campo usted   *Living in the country, you*
  no lo habría sabido.   *would not have known that.*
Con todos estos problemas   *With all these problems, you*
  tú te habrías vuelto loco   *would have gone mad too.*
  también.

exercise

**Use the conditional perfect to disassociate yourself from
someone else's actions.**

E.g. Julio compró un elefante. → Yo no lo habría comprado.

a Luisa se acostó tarde.
b Usted fumó muchos cigarrillos.
c Emilio y Juanita se casaron.
d Dormiste toda la tarde.
e Juan estudió inglés en la universidad.
f Lo creíste.
g Andrés se bañó en el mar.
h Ustedes dijeron la verdad.
i Julio se puso la mejor camisa.
j El prisionero se volvió loco.

The passive is used to make the direct object of an action the subject of the sentence.

A The passive is not used as commonly in Spanish as in English; nevertheless it is used in fairly formal style.

• active
Mucha gente lee este periódico.   *Many people read this newspaper.*

• passive
Este periódico es leído por mucha gente.   *This newspaper is read by many people.*

B The verb is made passive, as in English, by using the verb **ser** (*to be*) (see Unit 41) and a past participle (see Unit 59). The person bringing about the action is shown by **por** *by*.

La puerta es cerrada por el profesor.   *The door is closed by the teacher.*

Los ladrones fueron cogidos por la policía.   *The robbers were caught by the police.*

In this construction after **ser**, the past participle agrees in gender and number with the subject, for example **la puerta, los ladrones**.

C Spanish tends to avoid the passive by either using the normal active subject + verb + object or by using a reflexive verb with **se**.

Aquí se habla español.   *Spanish is spoken here.*

| Después del robo el dinero se escondió en un armario. | *After the robbery the money was hidden in a cupboard.* |

D The word order is fairly flexible, but the verb frequently comes in front of the subject: **se escondió el dinero** or **el dinero se escondió**. An article is required if a noun starts the expression: **Se habla inglés** but **el inglés se habla**.

| Los libros se devolvieron a la biblioteca. | *The books were returned to the library.* |
| Se vende pan en la panadería pero las legumbres se venden solamente en el mercado. | *Bread is sold in the baker's, but vegetables are sold only in the market.* |

NB If **por** is used to show the agent responsible, correct style requires the **ser** construction instead of **se**.

| Los libros fueron devueltos por los estudiantes. | *The books were returned by the students.* |
| Las legumbres son vendidas por los granjeros solamente en el mercado. | *Vegetables are sold by the farmers only in the market.* |

See exercise 30 in 'More practice'.

Spanish uses a special set of verb endings in different tenses to denote actions which are connected with or depend on another person's attitude.

A Look at the present subjunctive of the following verbs.

hablar	comer	escribir
hable	coma	escriba
hables	comas	escribas
hable	coma	escriba
hablemos	comamos	escribamos
habléis	comáis	escribáis
hablen	coman	escriban

Note that -er and -ir verbs have the same endings. You can see that in the present subjunctive verbs ending in -ar and -er/-ir have swapped endings compared with the ordinary present tense.

B Normally when one verb depends on another, you combine them using an infinitive, as in **quiero trabajar** *I want to work*; **prefieres descansar** *you prefer to rest*. However, the subjunctive is used after **que** if the subject changes.

Yo quiero trabajar.   *I want to work.*
(Yo) quiero que (tú) trabajes.   *I want you to work.*
Julio prefiere escribir la carta.   *Julio prefers to write the letter.*

Julio prefiere que nosotros escribamos la carta.

Julio prefers us to write the letter.

C When person B's (the second subject after **que**, known as the 'subordinate' clause) action is linked with person A's (the subject in the 'main' clause) attitude, replace the infinitive with **que** and a subjunctive.

No me gusta que usted hable inglés.

I don't like you speaking English.

Prohíben que comamos los caramelos.

They forbid us to eat the sweets.

NB Only use the subjunctive in the 'subordinate' clauses.

These verbs express emotion and opinion; they also need a subjunctive after **que**: esperar *to hope*; desear *to desire*; me gusta *I like*; preferir *to prefer*; insistir (en) *to insist*; mandar *to order*; necesitar *to need*.

exercise

Fill the gaps with the appropriate subjunctive verb from the box.

a Juan necesita que nosotros _____ en su jardín.

b Luisa y Ana prefieren que los chicos no _____ .

c Deseamos que ustedes _____ la carta ahora.

d No me gusta que tú _____ en la casa.

e ¿Esperas que Luisa _____ ?

f Esperamos que vosotros _____ bien.

---

cante descanséis escriban fumes griten trabajemos

Verbs which show some irregularity in the ordinary present tense usually repeat that change in the subjunctive.

A The root or base of the present subjunctive is the first person singular of the present tense. Look what happens with verbs whose first person present ends in -**go**, like **tengo** and **salgo**.

tener *to have*: tenga, tengas, tenga, tengamos, tengáis, tengan
salir *to go out*: salga, salgas, salga, salgamos, salgáis, salgan

No me gusta que Juan tenga cerveza.
I don't like Juan to have beer.
Quiere que salgas.
He wants you to go out.

Verbs similarly affected include: oír *to hear* → oiga; venir *to come* → venga; hacer *to do, make* → haga; decir *to say, tell* → diga; poner *to put* → ponga.

Necesito que digas la verdad. *I need you to tell the truth.*
Su madre quiere que se ponga un traje.
His mother wants him to put on a suit.

B Most radical-changing verbs make the same changes in the present subjunctive as in the ordinary present tense.

contar *to count*: cuente, cuentes, cuente, contemos, contéis, cuenten
perder *to lose*: pierda, pierdas, pierda, perdamos, perdáis, pierdan

C Now look at what happens to that group of radical-changing verbs in **-ir** like **pedir** *to ask*; **divertirse** *to have a good time*; **dormir** *to sleep*:

pedir: pida, pidas, pida, pidamos, pidáis, pidan

divertirse: me divierta, te diviertas, se divierta, nos divirtamos, os divirtáis, se diviertan

dormir: duerma, duermas, duerma, durmamos, durmáis, duerman

D **Ver** *to see* and **ser** *to be* have similar forms.

ver: vea, veas, vea, veamos, veáis, vean
ser: sea, seas, sea, seamos, seáis, sean

E ir *to go*: vaya, vayas, vaya, vayamos, vayáis, vayan

F saber *to know*: sepa, sepas, sepa, sepamos, sepáis, sepan

exercise

Change the present tenses to the corresponding person and forms of the subjunctive.

E.g. pides → pidas

a tiene	**f** pone
b salimos	**g** cuentan
c vienes	**h** nos divertimos
d digo	**i** dormimos
e hacemos	**j** vemos

Spanish uses the subjunctive with a variety of expressions of attitude.

A The subjunctive is used with verbs of wanting like **querer**. It is similarly used with verbs of not wanting and others with negative connotations, such as **prohibir** *to forbid*; **odiar** *to hate*; **impedir** *to prevent*.

Prohíbo que fumes.	*I forbid to you to smoke.*
Odio que bebas tanto.	*I hate you drinking so much.*
Impedimos que entren.	*We prevent them entering.*

B Other expressions involving attitude, including **alegrarse de** *to be glad*; **sentir** *to regret, be sorry*; **temer / tener miedo de** *to be afraid* and **dudar** *to doubt* are followed by **que** and a subjunctive.

Me alegro de que vengas.	*I am glad you are coming.*
Siento que Julio no esté aquí.	*I am sorry that Julio is not here.*
Teme que los niños se caigan.	*He is afraid that the children may/will fall over.*
Dudo que podamos ir.	*I doubt that we can go.*

Lo siento *I'm sorry* drops the **lo** when followed by **que** and the subjunctive.

C Similarly **ser/estar** *to be* + adjective of emotion require a subjunctive.

Está contenta que no llueva. *She is pleased it's not raining.*

D Almost any 'impersonal' expression introduced by **es** and followed by **que** requires a subjunctive.

Es necesario que trabajemos. *It's necessary (that) we work.*
Es imprescindible que sepa. *It's essential that he knows.*
Es curioso que vayas. *It's curious that you are going.*

From the last two examples, you can see that **saber** and **ir** have irregular subjunctives in **sepa** (etc.) and **vaya**.

exercise

The answers in this crossword are all subjunctive verbs.

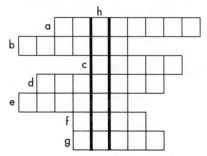

a Quiero que el niño (descansar).
b Es necesario que tú (hablar) español.
c Espero que Julio (poder) venir.
d Es necesario que nosotros (decir) la verdad.
e Ellos esperan que Luisa (dormir) bien.
f La madre quiere que el niño (comer) mucho.
g Me alegro que tú (estar) aquí.
h Es importante que nosotros (saber) nadar.

Spanish uses the subjunctive in subordinate clauses when the event has not yet happened or is in doubt.

A The subjunctive is often used after words such as **cuando** *when*, **tan pronto como** *as soon as*, **mientras** *while* and **hasta que** *until*.

Iré a la playa cuando Julio venga.	*I shall go to the beach when Julio comes.*
Cuando termines el desayuno puedes salir.	*When you finish your breakfast you can go out.*
Tan pronto como usted me diga la verdad estaré contento.	*As soon as you tell me the truth I shall be happy.*
Cuando gane la lotería voy a comprar un coche.	*When I win the lottery I shall buy a car.*
Te miraré mientras subas.	*I'll watch you while you go up.*
Esperaremos aquí hasta que lleguen.	*We shall wait here until they arrive.*

In all the above examples the speaker does not know for certain if they will be told the truth or if they will win the lottery or not – the actions referred to are all some time in the future.

Notice that verbs like **llegar** insert a **u** before the endings of the subjunctive to preserve the hard **g** sound. Verbs like **comenzar** and **empezar** change the **z** to **c**.

Jugaremos hasta que empiece a llover.	*We shall play until it starts raining.*

B The expression **antes (de) que** *before* always takes a subjunctive verb, as the event referred to has obviously not yet happened!

Vamos a salir antes (de) que   *Let's leave before they see us*
   nos vean.   *(they have not seen us yet!)*

C There does not need to be a change of subject for these expressions of futurity to require a subjunctive.

Trabajaré hasta que termine.   *I shall work until I finish.*
Cantarán hasta que mueran.   *They will sing until they die.*

However, if there is no change of subject, it is also possibe to use **hasta** + infinitive or **antes de** + infinitive:

Trabajaré hasta terminar.   *I shall work until I finish.*
Cantarán hasta morir.   *They will sing until they die.*
Terminaré el libro antes de   *I shall finish the book before*
   salir.   *going out.*

exercise

Translate the following into Spanish.

a We shall sing until the children leave.
b Luisa is going to rest until Julio comes.
c I shall buy a big house when I win the lottery.
d As soon as your father comes, we will eat.
e They will be happy when you tell the truth.
f We are going to swim until it starts raining.

Conditional sentences explain what someone would do or be if something happened. Spanish uses different constructions with si (if).

Spanish makes a distinction between a genuine possibility (*If it rains, I'll go in*), and an imaginary or hypothetical situation (*If I were rich, I would buy a car*).

A Si with genuine possibilities.
Spanish uses the same construction as English. Si is usually followed by the ordinary present tense. The main clause may be in the present or future tense.

Si tengo tiempo, voy al cine.	*If I have time, I go to the cinema.*
Si tengo tiempo, iré al cine mañana.	*If I have time, I'll go to the cinema tomorrow.*
Yo trabajaré si tú trabajas también.	*I'll work if you work too.*
Voy a ver la televisión si hay un programa bueno.	*I'm going to watch television if there's a good programme.*

B When it refers to an imaginary situation or something which is contrary to fact, si is followed by a past subjunctive – see Unit 73 (typically the imperfect subjunctive) and the main clause is in the conditional tense.

Si (yo) viviese / viviera en Madrid hablaría español.	*If I lived in Madrid, I would speak Spanish.*

| Si tú comieses / comieras pescado te daría sardinas. | *If you ate fish I would give you sardines.* |
| Compraríamos un coche nuevo si tuviésemos / tuviéramos dinero. | *We would buy a new car if we had the money.* |

C The subjunctive is also used when the *if* refers to as yet unfulfilled conditions in the past.

| El ladrón dijo que mataría a la chica si no le diese / diera el dinero. | *The robber said he would kill the girl if she didn't give him the money.* |
| Si yo fuese / fuera el profesor estaría muy enfadado. | *If I were the teacher I'd be very cross.* |

Use a past subjunctive, never the present subjunctive, after si.

D In literary or formal style it is possible to use the -ra form of the subjunctive in both parts of the sentence.

| Si tuviera dinero comprara un coche. | *If I had the money I would buy a car.* |

exercise

Select the correct form according to the context.

E.g. Si tengo/tuviese tiempo, iría al cine. → tuviese

a Si Juan viene/viniese vamos a nadar.

b Si tengo/tuviera hijos compraré una casa más grande.

c Si tenemos/tuviésemos tiempo, visitaríamos a la familia.

d Si estoy/estuviera enfermo, llamaría al médico.

Spanish has many ways of expressing possibility. This unit looks at the most important ones.

A Es posible que *It's possible that, It may / might* – like other 'impersonal expressions' – is followed by the subjunctive.

Es posible que llueva.	*It's possible it will rain / it might rain.*
No es cierto que venga.	*It's not certain he'll come.*
Es dudoso que haya un tren.	*It's doubtful there's a train.*

B There are many ways of expressing *perhaps* in Spanish.

• **Puede ser que** + subjunctive *perhaps, maybe*

Puede ser que no llegue a tiempo.	*Maybe he won't arrive in time.*

• **Tal vez, acaso, quizás, quizá** (*perhaps*) are all usually followed by the subjunctive.

Acaso no tengamos que pagar.	*Perhaps we don't / won't have to pay.*
Quizás haya una gasolinera por aquí.	*Perhaps there is a petrol station round here.*
Quizá el perro no muerda.	*Perhaps the dog won't bite.*

C These expressions are sometimes followed by a non-subjunctive verb to imply a greater degree of certainty.

Tal vez el profesor comprende – es un hombre simpático.	*Perhaps the teacher will understand – he's a nice man.*
Quizás te veremos a la hora de comer.	*Perhaps we'll see you at lunchtime.*

D You can avoid a subjunctive by putting the **quizá** (etc.) at the end of the sentence.

Te veremos pronto, quizá.　　*We'll see you soon, perhaps.*

E A lo mejor *perhaps* is a useful expression which never takes the subjunctive. It is not as strong as **quizás**, etc. and can (but does not necessarily) suggest optimism.

A lo mejor encontramos una　*Perhaps we'll get a room here.*
　habitación aquí.

A lo mejor tendremos mejor　*Perhaps we'll have a better*
　día mañana.　　　　　　　　*day tomorrow.*

exercise

Translate the following into Spanish.

a It is possible it will rain today.
b It is probable that he won't come.
c Maybe Pedro will write soon.
d It's doubtful we have enough money.
e It is not certain that we can go.
f Perhaps he will arrive tomorrow.
g He will arrive tomorrow, perhaps.
h Perhaps the nice man will pay!
i Perhaps he understands Spanish.
j Perhaps you'll feel better soon.

Spanish can reflect certainty or uncertainty by choosing to use the subjunctive or not in a variety of contexts.

A **Aunque** *although, even though* is followed by the appropriate (non-subjunctive) tense when stating a fact.

Aunque es tarde, el sol brilla todavía.	*Although it is late, the sun is still shining.*
Bebe mucho aunque no tiene mucho dinero.	*He drinks a lot even though he does not have much money.*
Vamos a nadar aunque llueve mucho.	*We are going swimming even though it is raining hard.*

B **Aunque** *even if* is followed by a subjunctive verb.

Aunque llueva mucho, vamos a nadar.	*We are going swimming even if it rains hard.*
No les daré el dinero aunque tengan pistola.	*I shall not give them the money even if they have guns.*
Dijo que no saldría con Julio aunque la invitase / invitara.	*She said she would not go out with Julio even if he invited her.*

C Many other situations use the subjunctive rather than the ordinary ('indicative') tenses in a subordinate or secondary clause with an unknown or hypothetical subject.

Toma el libro que quieres.	*Take the book (= specific book) you want.*
Toma el libro que quieras.	*Take the book (= whichever one) you want.*

Buscamos al mecánico que repara coches.	*We are looking for the mechanic (a specific person) who repairs cars.*
Buscamos un mecánico que repare coches.	*We are looking for a mechanic (= any one) who repairs cars.*

D **Ojalá** *if only* is followed by a subjunctive. It refers to an event which is contrary to fact or not yet certain. In the present it is often followed by **que**.

Ojalá (que) gane la lotería esta vez.	*If only I win the lottery this time.*
Ojalá hablase / hablara inglés.	*If only I spoke English.*

Ojalá is also used as a one-word answer.

¿Estás de vacaciones? ¡Ojalá!	*Are you on holiday? If only! / I wish! / You must be joking!*, etc.

exercise

Practise using *aunque*: choose the indicative or subjunctive according to the context.

a Te comprendo aunque no hablas/hables español.

b Voy a continuar trabajando aunque gano/gane la lotería.

c Aunque es/sea difícil, nos gusta estudiar el latín.

d Aunque Madrid es/sea grande es muy bonito.

e No te daré el dinero aunque me lo pides/pidieses.

The subjunctive is used for all negative commands and for polite positive commands.

A You will often see polite commands on public transport, formal notices or in adverts. These use the **usted** (singular) and **ustedes** (plural) forms of the subjunctive.

Tenga cuidado.	*Take care.*
Suban y bajen rápidamente.	*Get on and off quickly.*
No pisen la hierba.	*Don't walk on the grass.*
Tiren; Empujen	*Pull; Push*

With strangers it is polite to add **usted** or **ustedes**.

Perdóneme usted.	*Excuse me.*

B The object or reflexive pronoun goes on the end of positive commands but before all negative commands.

Siéntese	*Sit down.*
Quítese el abrigo.	*Take off your coat.*
¿Dígame? / ¿Diga?	*Hello?* (on the phone)
¡No me digas! ¡No me diga!	*You don't say!*
No se moleste usted.	*Don't bother yourself.*
No te preocupes / No se preocupe.	*Don't worry.*

C You can also give a command by using the verb **querer** *to want* with an infinitive. This can sound less abrupt.

¿Quiere usted darme un kilo de patatas?	*Will you give me a kilo of potatoes?*

D There are also some rather formal expressions which use the polite commands of **tener** *to have* and **hacer** *to do, make*: **tenga(n)** and **haga(n)** with an infinitive.

Tenga la bondad de pagar la cuenta.	*Have the goodness to pay the bill.*
Haga el favor de mantener silencio después de las once.	*Do the favour of observing silence after 11.*

E In instruction leaflets and notices, the infinitive is often used as a command.

Abrir el paquete y meter el contenido en una sartén.	*Open the packet and put the contents in a pan.*
No aparcar.	*No parking.*

exercise

Make these commands negative. Remember to change the word order and remove any unnecessary accents.

E.g. Preocúpese. → No se preocupe.

a Moléstese.
b Lávese.
c Ábrala.
d Ciérrela.
e Dígame.

f Págueme.
g Siéntense.
h Póngaselo.
i Quítenselo.

Tú and **vosotros**, the familar forms singular and plural for *you*, form their positive commands using the 'true imperative'.

A **Tú** positive commands are usually formed by dropping the final -s from the **tú** form of the present tense: hablar → habla; comer → come; escribir → escribe

Habla español.	*Speak Spanish.*
Come más.	*Eat more.*
Escribe una carta.	*Write a letter.*

B As with formal positive commands, any object or reflexive pronouns join on the end, adding an accent on the stressed syllable.

Levántate.	*Get up.*
Escríbeme pronto.	*Write to me soon.*

C A few verbs have irregular short **tú** imperatives: poner *to put* → pon; hacer *to do, make* → haz; decir *to say* → di; salir *to go out* → sal; ser *to be* → sé; tener *to have* → ten; venir *to come* → ven; ir *to go* → ve.

Ven conmigo.	*Come with me.*
Ten cuidado.	*Take care.*
Pon la mesa.	*Lay the table.*
Dime la verdad.	*Tell me the truth.*

Note that **ve** is also the regular **tú** imperative from **ver** *to see*.

An accent is only required with more than one object pronoun.

Póntelo.	*Put it on.*	Dímelo.	*Tell me it.*

D The **vosotros** (familiar plural) imperative is even simpler. Just change the final -r of the infinitive to -d: hablar → hablad; decir → decid; hacer → haced; escribir → escribid; comer → comed; tener → tened.

There are no exceptions, so **ir** (*to go*) → **id**; **ser** (*to be*) → **sed**.

E Reflexive verbs, however, drop the **d** in front of the reflexive pronoun **os**, except with **irse** *to go away*: **lavaos** *get washed*; **levantaos** *get up*; **vestíos** *get dressed* (from **vestir**); **divertíos** *have a good time* (from **divertirse**), but **idos** *go away*.

Remember all *negative* commands are formed from the subjunctive: see Unit 71.

exercise

Give the *tú* and *vosotros* imperatives of these verbs.

E.g. comer → come → comed

a beber
b hablar
c escribir
d vivir
e correr

Give the *tú* and *vosotros* imperatives of these reflexive verbs. Don't forget to add any necessary accent.

E.g. lavarse → lávate → lavaos

f levantarse (*to get up*)
g acostarse (*to go to bed*)
h vestirse (*to get dressed*)
i dormirse (*to fall asleep*)
j esconderse (*to hide*)

The subjunctive is used in past tenses as well as the present. This unit explains the most commonly used past tense, the imperfect subjunctive.

73 subjunctive: past tenses

A The present subjunctive is used in a subordinate clause when the main clause refers to present or future time. If the main clause is in the past, the subjunctive will also be in the past.

No quiero que trabajes.   *I don't want you to work.*
No quería que trabajases.   *I didn't want you to work.*

In this sentence, **trabajases** is a past subjunctive.

B The good news is that one past tense of the subjunctive – the imperfect – serves a number of contexts. Even better news is that all verbs form this tense in the same way. The bad news is that, in modern Spanish, there are two alternative sets of endings. In practice, you use either!

hablar		comer	
hablase	hablara	comiese	comiera
hablases	hablaras	comieses	comieras
hablase	hablara	comiese	comiera
hablásemos	habláramos	comiésemos	comiéramos
hablaseis	hablarais	comieseis	comierais
hablasen	hablaran	comiesen	comieran

The imperfect subjunctive is formed from the **ellos / ellas** form of the preterite (**hablaron, comieron** etc.): take off the **-ron** and add either a **-se** or a **-ra** set of endings.

NB All the **nosotros** forms have an accent: **hablásemos**, etc.

C There are no irregular endings; all verbs form their imperfect subjunctives in the same way, from the preterite: ir / ser (fueron) → fuese / fuera, etc.; decir (dijeron) → dijese / dijera, etc.; hacer (hicieron) → hiciese / hiciera.

exercise

Put these sentences into the past, using the imperfect subjunctive after *que*.

E.g. Juan quiere que Luisa hable. → Juan quería que Luisa hablase/ hablara.

a Juan quiere que Luisa coma. Juan quería …

b Queremos que los niños trabajen. Queríamos …

c El profesor prohíbe que el estudiante entre. El profesor prohibió …

d Los estudiantes quieren que el profesor salga. Los estudiantes querían …

e Prefiero que usted no fume. Prefería …

f Es imposible que Julio llegue. Era imposible …

g Me gusta que cante. Me gustaba …

h Preferimos que no bebáis. Preferíamos …

Sometimes we need to put two verbs together. This and following units show how this done.

A How Spanish verbs are joined depends on the verb being used. Many verbs combine simply as in English, with the first verb being directly followed by an infinitive.

Quiero descansar.	*I want to rest.*
Deben decidir.	*They must decide.*
No puedes salir mañana.	*You cannot go out tomorrow.*

B Common verbs followed directly by the infinitive include:

conseguir/lograr *to succeed, manage*
deber *must, should*
decidir *to decide*
dejar/permitir *to allow*
desear/querer *to want, desire*
esperar *to expect, hope, wait*
hacer *to make*
impedir *to prevent*
intentar *to try*
mandar *to order*
necesitar *to need*

ofrecer *to offer*
olvidar *to forget*
pensar *to intend*
poder *to be able*
preferir *to prefer*
prohibir *to forbid*
prometer *to promise*
recordar *to remember, remind*
rehusar *to refuse*
saber *to know how*
soler *to be accustomed*
temer *to be afraid*

Conseguí entrar por la ventana.	*I managed to get in through the window.*
Nos prohíben ver la película.	*They forbid us to see the film.*

Prefiero quedarme en casa. *I prefer to stay at home.*
Has olvidado enviar la carta. *You have forgotten to send the letter.*

C Verbs of perception such as **oír** *to hear*, **ver** *to see* and **sentir** *to feel, hear* are also followed by the infinitive, whereas English uses -ing.

Los oímos jugar en el patio. *We heard them playing in the yard.*

La veo tocar el piano. *I see her playing the piano.*
Te siento correr por el pasillo. *I hear / perceive you running down the corridor.*

exercise

Practise linking with *querer* (to want), *deber* (must, should), *poder* (can, be able), *pensar* (to intend), *preferir* (to prefer), *olvidar* (to forget), *decidir* (to decide).

E.g. I want to read (leer). → Quiero leer.

a He wants to eat (**comer**).

b I prefer to rest (**descansar**).

c They decide to buy (**comprar**).

d You cannot go out today (**salir hoy**).

e We must study (**estudiar**).

f They forget to write (**escribir**).

g Do you intend to go (**ir**)?

Some verbs are not linked directly. This deals with verbs that are joined with *a*.

A All verbs of motion take **a** before an infinitive.

Voy a comer pan.	*I'm going to eat bread.*
Corrieron a ayudarme.	*They ran to help me.*
¿Salimos a pasear?	*Are we going out for a walk?*
Julio viene a cenar.	*Julio is coming to have supper.*

Similarly **bajar** *to go down(stairs)*, **subir** *to go up(stairs)*, **entrar** *to go in*, **llegar** *to arrive*, etc.

B **A** may be changed to **para** if you want to emphasize the purpose.

Salieron para ayudarle.	*They went out (in order) to help him.*

C Verbs of beginning, such as **empezar**, **comenzar**, **ponerse** and **echar(se)**, are also followed by **a**.

Empiezo a estudiar.	*I begin to study.*
Comienzo a leer.	*I start to read.*
Me pongo a escribir.	*I start to write.*
(Me) echo a reír.	*I start to laugh.*

D Verbs which may be considered as equivalent to beginning or causing to begin are usually followed by **a**: aprender *to learn*; atreverse *to dare*; acostumbrarse *to get accustomed*; animar *to encourage*; dedicarse *to go in for, devote oneself to*; enseñar *to show, teach*; invitar *to invite*; obligar *to force*; persuadir *to persuade*; prepararse *to get ready*; volver *to do again, to re-*.

Aprendieron a nadar.	*They learned to swim.*
Julio la invita a salir.	*Julio invites her to go out.*
Volvimos a leer el libro.	*We re-read the book.*

E Although **decidir** *to decide* is followed by a direct infinitive (see Unit 74), **decidirse** is followed by **a** and tends to show greater emphasis.

Me decidí a aprender a conducir.	*I made up my mind to learn to drive.*

exercise

Practice using verbs of motion.

E.g. Escribo una carta (ir). → Voy a escribir una carta.

a Tocamos el piano (ir).

b Paseo en el parque (salir).

Use *a* with verbs of beginning.

E.g. I begin to read (ponerse). → Me pongo a leer.

c He begins to read (comenzar).

d We start to write (empezar).

Use *a* with verbs of learning and teaching or causing to do something.

E.g. I'm learning to swim (aprender). → Aprendo a nadar.

e Luisa is learning to swim (aprender).

f Julio is studying to be a mechanic (estudiar).

g He forces us to rest (obligar).

h We invite you to eat (invitar).

This unit looks at verbs that require *de* before an infinitive.

A Verbs suggesting the end of an action or an event all tend to require **de** before an infinitive. These include **terminar** *to finish* and **dejar** *to stop, give up*.

Terminó de leer.	*He stopped reading.*
He dejado de fumar.	*I have given up smoking.*

Acabar, literally *to bring to an end*, followed by **de** means *to have just* + infinitive (see Unit 79).

Acabo de recibir la carta.	*I have just received the letter.*

B Similarly, verbs looking back on an action or event are often followed by **de**: arrepentirse *to repent, regret*; avergonzarse *to be ashamed*; jactarse *to boast*; presumir *to show off, make a show*; preocuparse *to worry*; cuidar *to take care*; encargarse *to take charge*; tratar *to try*.

Me arrepiento de comprarlo.	*I regret buying it.*
Se avergüenza de reír.	*He is ashamed of laughing.*
Nos jactamos de ganar el premio.	*We boast of winning the prize.*
Luisa presume de conducir su coche nuevo.	*Luisa makes a show of driving her new car.*
Siempre me preocupo de conocer a gente nueva.	*I always worry about meeting new people.*
El portero se cuidó de aparcar el coche.	*The doorman took care of parking the car.*

Me encargué de escoger el vino. *I took charge of choosing the wine.*

Tratamos de dormir, pero sin éxito. *We tried to sleep, but without success.*

C Although **recordar** *to remember* is followed by a direct infinitive, **acordarse** *to remember* is followed by **de**. Similarly, **olvidarse** (*to forget*) requires **de**.

Julio nunca se acuerda de cerrar los grifos. *Julio never remembers to turn off the taps.*

No se olvide de despertarnos. *Don't forget to wake us.*

exercise

Fill the gaps with the appropriate verb with *de* from the box.

a El portero _____ de abrir la puerta.

b Julio no _____ de llamarme por teléfono.

c Yo _____ de comprar un coche.

d Siempre _____ de estudiar pero no puedo.

e Los niños _____ de ganar el partido de fútbol.

f Luisa _____ de conducir su coche rápido.

g No gracias, _____ de fumar.

h ¡Ay! ¡_____ de cerrar los grifos!

---

he dejado   me arrepentí   me he olvidado   presume
se acordó   se encargó   se jactaron   trato

Although *a* and *de* are the most common linking prepositions with an infinitive, some verbs take other prepositions.

A Verbs of struggling, such as **luchar** (*to fight, struggle*) and **esforzarse** (*to make an effort, strive*), are followed by **por**.

Luchamos por conseguir una entrada.	*We fought to get a ticket.*
Me esfuerzo por aprobar el examen.	*I make an effort to pass the exam.*

B Some verbs are used with **en** before an infinitive: consentir *to consent, agree*; dudar/vacilar *to hesitate*; empeñarse *to be determined*; insistir *to insist*; interesarse *to be interested*; quedar *to agree, arrange*; tardar *to take time*.

Consentimos en prestarle el dinero.	*We agreed to lend him the money.*
Dudó en contestar.	*He hesitated to reply.*
Me empeño en terminar el libro.	*I'm determined to finish the book.*
Los amigos quedaron en reunirse a las seis.	*The friends agreed/arranged to meet at six.*
El tren tarda dos horas en llegar a Madrid.	*The train takes two hours to get to Madrid.*

Note that **interesarse** can also be followed by **por**.

C A few verbs are followed by **con**: amenazar *to threaten*; contar *to rely, count on*; soñar *to dream*.

Los vecinos amenazaron con llamar a la policía.	*The neighbours threatened to call the police.*
Siempre cuenta con encontrar trabajo.	*He always relies on finding work.*
Sueño con ganar la lotería.	*I dream of winning the lottery.*

NB Verbs of continuing, **continuar** and **seguir**, do not take an infinitive, unlike English, but are followed by the gerund.

Continúa leyendo.	*He continues to read.*

exercise

Fill the gaps with the appropriate preposition.

a El cantante consiente _____ cantar.

b El público se esfuerza _____ oír.

c Luchamos _____ ganar la victoria.

d Dudamos _____ pagar la cuenta.

e Los ladrones siempre cuentan _____ encontrar dinero.

f Insisto _____ pagar el vino.

g ¿Cuánto tiempo tardas _____ leer un libro?

h Los ingleses sueñan _____ tomar el sol.

This unit looks at *haber* (to have) used in a special way.

A The verb *to have* (*possess*) is **tener**.

Tengo dos hijos.	*I have two children.*
No tenemos tiempo para hacerlo.	*We haven't got time to do it.*

Haber *to have* is not used in the sense of *to possess*, but has two other main uses.

• To form compound tenses as in English.

He comprado un coche.	*I have bought a car.*
¿Habías bebido todo el vino?	*Had you drunk all the wine?*

• As an expression corresponding to the English *there is* or *there are*, when describing a scene or a situation. In this use, **haber** is only used in the third person singular. In the present tense alone, it adds **y** (**hay**).

• **hay** (present): *there is / are*

¿Hay servicios por aquí?	*Are there any toilets round here?*

• **había** (imperfect): *there was / were / used to be*

En España había muchos burros.	*In Spain there used to be a lot of donkeys.*

• **hubo** (preterite): *there was*

De repente hubo una llamada en la puerta	*Suddenly there was a knock at the door.*

- **ha habido** (present perfect): *there has/have been*
  Ha habido muchas huelgas   *There have been a lot of*
    recientemente.   *strikes lately.*
- **había habido** (pluperfect): *there had been*
  Había habido un accidente.   *There had been an accident.*
- **habrá** (future): *there will be*
  Mañana habrá una corrida.   *There will be a bullfight*
                                                      tomorrow.
- **va a haber** (future): *there is going to be*
  Va a haber una guerra.   *There is going to be a war.*
- **habría** (conditional): *there would be*

  Habría muchos candidatos   *There would be many*
    para el trabajo.   *candidates for the job.*

B Purists avoid **hay** with the definite article, preferring **existe** instead.

  Existe la posibilidad de lluvia. *There is the possibility of rain.*

C **Hay que** plus an infinitive suggests a general requirement for action.

  Para ganar hay que jugar.   *You've got to play in order to*
                                                      win.

  Hay que trabajar mucho aquí. *One has to work hard here.*

See exercise 37 in 'More practice'.

Spanish has two useful idiomatic constructions to express past and future actions using *acabar* and *volver*.

A **Acabar** on its own means *to finish, end* or *to be over*.

La palabra acaba por s.	*The word ends in s.*
Ha acabado la tarea.	*He has finished the task.*
La fiesta acabó.	*The party was over.*

Acabar de plus an infinitive means *to have just …*

Acabo de leer la carta.	*I have just read the letter.*
Juan acaba de salir.	*Juan has just left.*
Acabamos de ver el dinero.	*We have just seen the money.*

B **Acabar de** is used in the present tense when it refers to an action that has just happened. If you refer to a past event, **acabar de** is put in the imperfect tense (see Unit 54).

Acababa de leer la carta.	*I had just read the letter.*
Juan acababa de salir.	*Juan had just left.*
Acabábamos de ver el dinero.	*We had just seen the money.*

It is unlikely that you will use **acabar de** in any tense other than the present or imperfect.

C **Volver** on its own means *to return*.

Mañana volvemos a Madrid.	*Tomorrow we are returning to Madrid.*
Julio volvió al día siguiente.	*Julio came back the following day.*

Remember that *return* (*give back*) is **devolver.**

Julio devolvió el dinero. *Julio gave back the money.*

Volver a plus an infinitive means *to (do) again.*
Vuelvo a leer la carta. *I'm reading the letter again.*
Julio volvió a llamar. *Julio called again.*
La besé y luego la volví a besar. *I kissed her then kissed her again.*

D **Volver** can be used in any tense the context demands.
Todos los días volvía a tocar el disco. *Every day I would play the record again.*
Después de media hora volvió a llover. *Half an hour later it rained again.*

exercise

Express the person's enthusiasm for the action which follows, using *acabar de* and *volver a* plus infinitives.

E.g. yo (cantar) → Yo acabo de cantar pero vuelvo a cantar en seguida.

a yo (comer)
b usted (nadar)
c Julio (cantar)
d nosotros (leer)
e ellos (jugar al tenis)

f tú (salir)
g los señores García (llamar)
h tú (hacer una paella)
i nosotros (ir a la ciudad)
j ustedes (escribir)

Spanish has two principal ways of saying *to know*.

saber *to know (have learned)*	conocer *to know, be acquainted with*
sé	conozco
sabes	conoces
sabe	conoce
sabemos	conocemos
sabéis	conocéis
saben	conocen

A **Saber** is used to know about something.

Sabemos que España es muy bonita.	*We know that Spain is very pretty.*
No sé dónde está el banco.	*I don't know where the bank is.*

B **Conocer** is used to express familiarity. **Reconocer** means *to recognize* (i.e. come across again).

¿Quién es Luisa? No la conozco.	*Who is Luisa? I don't know her. (i.e. I have never met her.)*
Me gusta la paella ¿Tú la conoces?	*I like paella. Have you come across it?*
Este verano esperamos conocer Extremadura. ¿La conoces?	*This summer we are hoping to get to know Extremadura. Do you know (of) it?*
BUT	
¿Tú sabes algo de Extremadura?	*Do you know anything about Extremadura? (Is it big, hot, fertile?, etc.)*

Never follow **conocer** with **que**: use **saber** in such cases.

Sí, sé que Extremadura es una   *Yes, I know (that)*
región en el oeste de España.   *Extremadura is a region
                                 in the west of Spain.*

C In the preterite tense (see Unit 51), **conocer** has the force of
to have met.

Conocí a Julio en Madrid.   *I met (= made the acquaintance
                             of) Julio in Madrid.*

NB The adjective/past participle **conocido** means *famous.*

La paella valenciana es   *The paella they make in
conocida por su riqueza.   Valencia is famous for being
                             tasty.*

exercise

Fill the gaps with the correct form of either *saber* or *conocer*.

E.g. **a** Julio _____ Granada porque su familia vive allí.
b Luisa _____ que Granada es una ciudad muy histórica.
c Julio _____ a Luisa: son colegas.
d Yo no _____ a Luisa, pero es una escritora conocida.
e Yo no _____ nada de Julio. ¿Es conocido?
f Claro que sí. Tú le _____ desde niño.

Spanish makes a distinction between *can* when it means ability, knowledge or permission.

A In English we use *can* in a variety of ways, for example, *I can swim*; *You can't swim because you have not brought your costume*; *Can you park here?*; *Can you speak Spanish?*

B *To be able* can be expressed by **poder** or **saber**. Both verbs have some points to note in their present tenses.

poder *to be able, can*	saber *to know (how), can*
puedo	sé
puedes	sabes
puede	sabe
podemos	sabemos
podéis	sabéis
pueden	saben

Poder is used for a practical or physical possibility.

Puedo comprar un coche porque tengo mucho dinero.	*I can buy a car because I have a lot of money.*
No podemos nadar hoy porque la piscina está cerrada.	*We can't swim today because the pool is closed.*
Luis no puede hablar porque tiene la boca llena.	*Luis can't speak because his mouth is full.*

For a general statement of permission, use **se puede**.

¿Se puede fumar aquí?	*Can you / one smoke here?*

C Saber (= *to know*) is used if the ability depends on experience or learning.

¡Socorro! ¡No sé nadar! *Help! I can't swim!*

¿Sabes hablar español? *Can you speak Spanish?*

Compare:

Este pobre muchacho no sabe escribir. *This poor boy can't write (i.e. he's illiterate).*

Este pobre muchacho no puede escribir. *This poor boy can't write (i.e. he doesn't have pencil and paper).*

exercise

Insert the correct form of *poder* or *saber* as required.

a Estoy perdido. ¿_____ usted ayudarme?

b No _____ abrir la puerta. Está cerrada.

c Luisa, ¿tú _____ nadar esta tarde?

d Me gusta mucho estar en la playa, pero no _____ nadar.

e No se _____ aparcar en el centro de la ciudad.

f No _____ leer este libro porque no tengo mis gafas.

g No comprendo los periódicos porque no _____ leer.

h Mi hermana _____ tocar el piano. En casa _____ practicar todos los días, pero en el colegio no _____ .

This unit looks at the various ways Spanish can say *to become*.

A Ponerse is commonly used with an adjective to describe a coincidental or involuntary physical or emotional change.

Julio se puso pálido al leer las noticias.	*Julio became (turned) pale when he read the news.*
Luisa se pone roja cuando habla conmigo.	*Luisa blushes (becomes red) when she speaks to me.*
Nosotros nos pusimos muy contentos al ver el premio.	*We became very happy when we saw the prize.*

B Volverse is used with an adjective to suggest a sudden, more profound or violent and permanent change.

Mi amigo se volvió loco.	*My friend went mad.*
¡No puedo más! ¡Me vuelvo loco!	*I can't take any more! I'm going mad!.*
Esos estudiantes se han vuelto imposibles – no quieren aprender nada.	*Those students have become impossible – they don't want to learn anything.*

C Hacerse is used with adjectives or nouns. It suggests intention linked to social or professional status.

Pedro se hizo cantante y se hizo rico.	*Pedro became a singer and became rich too.*
Tú y yo nos hicimos amigos.	*You and I became friends.*

D Llegar a ser suggests coincidence or lack of intention.

Juan Pérez llegó a ser presidente.	*Juan Pérez became president.*

E Reflexive verbs such as the following often express 'becoming' or 'getting': cansarse *to get tired*; enfadarse *to get angry*; enriquecerse *to get rich*; enfurecerse *to get furious*; emocionarse *to get excited*.

Los niños se cansaron de jugar.
The children got tired of playing!

¡No te enfades, papá! *Don't get angry, Dad!*

F A handful of verbs are not reflexive, although they refer to personal change: engordar *to get fat, put on weight*; adelgazar *to get thin, slim*; envejecer *to get old*; mejorar *to improve*; empeorar *to get worse*.

Has adelgazado – ¡no te reconocí!
I didn't recognize you – you've lost weight!

exercise

Translate the following into Spanish.

a She always becomes pale.
b They want to become rich.
c The students became teachers.
d My teacher became mad.
e I don't want to get fat.
f I get tired quickly.
g Pedro gets angry quickly.
h It's easy to get excited.
i We shall never become friends.
j They have become impossible.

Choosing the right verb in Spanish for *to leave* can cause problems. Here are some general hints.

A **Dejar** is used to mean *to leave something or someone behind*.

He dejado mi dinero en casa.	*I've left my money at home.*
¿Dónde dejaste las entradas?	*Where did you leave the tickets?*
¿Quieres dejarme en la estación?	*Will you drop me (off) at the station?*
¡Déjame en paz!	*Leave me alone! (= in peace)*

B **Dejar** plus an infinitive means *to allow, permit* (like the old English *by your leave*).

Tú nunca me dejas salir.	*You never let me go out.*

See also Unit 76: **dejar de** + infinitive = *to give up*.

C **Salir** means *to leave* in the sense of *to go out* and cannot take a direct object. Use **de** to show what you are leaving.

Salgo de casa a las ocho.	*I leave home at eight.*
El tren sale a las diez y media.	*The train leaves (= departs) at 10.30.*

D **Salir** plus an adjective or adverb often translates *to turn out*.

El concierto salió interesante.	*The concert turned out to be interesting.*
Todo va a salir bien.	*Everything will turn out fine.*

E **Irse** and **marcharse** can also mean *to leave* in the sense of *to go away.*

Nos vamos del trabajo a las dos.	*We're leaving work at 2.*

Marcharse can imply leaving forever or for a long time.

No me gusta este trabajo – me marcho.	*I don't like this job – I'm off!*

F **Abandonar**, besides meaning *to abandon*, as in English, can also be used with places.

Abandonó Madrid y fue a trabajar a Barcelona.	*He left Madrid and went to work in Barcelona.*

NB *Never* use the verb **quitar** in this context; unlike *to quit* or French *quitter*, **quitar** means *to steal* or *take away.*

Me quitaron el dinero.	*They pinched my money.*

exercise

Link the expressions to form as many sentences as possible.

Julio	siempre (*always*)	sale	las llaves en casa.
El tren	nunca (*never*)	deja	de la oficina.
El trabajo	a veces (*sometimes*)	se marcha	Barcelona.
	mañana (*tomorrow*)	se va	de Granada.
		abandona	tarde.
			bien.
			a su familia.

Spanish has a number of ways to say *to look*.

A Parecer = *to seem*

Me pareces muy bonita.	*You look very pretty to me.*
Al profesor el ejercicio no le pareció nada difícil.	*The exercise didn't seem at all difficult to the teacher.*

B Parecerse a = *to look like/resemble*

Juan se parece a su hermano. *Juan looks like his brother.*

C Mirar = *to look (at)*

Mira (**mire** in the **usted** form) is often used to direct attention.

Mira, Juan, está lloviendo.	*Look, Juan, it's raining.*
Mire usted, no podemos pagar tanto.	*Look, we can't pay as much as that.*

When it means *to look at* notice that *at* is not translated.

Quiero mirar este cuadro. *I want to look at this picture.*

Personal **a** is, however, required when the object of **mirar** is a specific person or persons.

Mira a tu padre – está dormido.	*Look at your father – he's asleep.*

NB *To watch TV, a film,* etc. is generally **ver la televisión, ver una película**.

D Buscar = *to look for, search*

The word *for* is not translated.

Siempre busco mis llaves. *I'm always looking for my keys.*

Busco a Juan.   *I'm looking for Juan.*
BUT
Busco un profesor de guitarra. *I need a guitar teacher.*

E **Tener cuidado** = *to look out / take care*
Tenga cuidado de no introducir   *Mind the gap (on Spanish*
el pie entre coche y andén.   *metro trains)*

A more idiomatic way of saying *look out* is with **ojo con** or **a**.
¡Ojo con/a los rateros!   *Beware of pickpockets.*

F **dar a** = *to look out over*
El hotel da al mar.   *The hotel looks out over the
                                 sea.*

G **Repasar** = *to look through (notes, newspaper, etc.)*
Tengo que repasar mis   *I must look through my
apuntes.   notes.*

exercise

**Solve the clues and then fit them into the grid. One is already
done for you.**

a Nosotros _____ el mar.
b ¿Qué te _____ Madrid?
c Se _____ piso.
d _____ con los rateros.
e Tenga _____
f Tengo que _____ mis
apuntes para el examen.

English uses the verb *to miss* in many different ways. This unit looks at suitable Spanish equivalents.

A **Perder** can mean *to miss* (transport).

Vamos a perder el tren.	*We're going to miss the train.*
Julio perdió el autobús.	*Julio missed the bus.*

Perder normally means *to lose*.

Perdí mi dinero en la playa. *I lost my money on the beach.*

B **Perderse** is used with entertainment or occasions.

No quiero perderme la película.	*I don't want to miss the film.*
Nos perdimos el concierto en el parque.	*We missed the concert in the park.*

C **Echar de menos** means *to miss* emotionally.

Echo de menos a mi familia.	*I miss my family.*
Los chicos echaban de menos a las chicas.	*The boys missed the girls.*

D **No entender** *to understand* and **no oír** *to hear* mean *to miss, not to catch* (of words, etc.).

No oímos lo que dijo. *We missed what he said.*

E **Errar, fallar el blanco** mean *to miss* in the sense of a target, etc.

Tiró pero erró / falló el blanco. *He fired but missed.*

F **Faltar** means *to be missing*. Watch out for the use of the indirect object pronoun in Spanish where English uses a possessive adjective.

Juanito faltaba a clase.   *Juanito missed school.*
Me falta el dinero – ¿dónde   *My money's missing – where*
   está?   *is it?*
Faltan tres estudiantes.   *Three students are missing.*

G **No dejar de** + infinitive translates *Don't miss …*
No dejes de visitar la   *Don't miss (visiting) the*
   catedral – es bonita.   *cathedral – it's lovely.*

exercise

Solve the crossword.

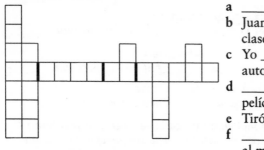

a _____, Luisa.
b Juanito _____ a clase.
c Yo _____ el autobús.
d _____ perdí la película.
e Tiró pero _____ .
f _____ dejes de ir al museo.

Spanish has a number of verbs to translate *to put*. This unit shows the main distinctions.

A **Poner** = *to put*. This verb may be used in most contexts.

Pone la revista en la mesa.	*He puts the magazine on the table.*

Poner has first person singular, present tense **pongo**, and is a **pretérito grave**.

Pongo la sartén en la cocina eléctrica.	*I put the frying pan on the stove.*
Puso la toalla en el estante.	*He put the towel on the shelf.*

B **Poner** = *to put on* (radio, TV, etc.)

Pon la tele, Juanito.	*Put the TV on, Juanito.*

C **Poner la mesa** = *to lay the table*

¿Quieres poner la mesa?	*Will you lay the table?*

D **Ponerse** = *to put on* (clothes, etc.)

Me puse el mejor traje.	*I put on my best suit.*

Ponerse can also mean *to get, become.*

Se pusieron nerviosos.	*They got nervous.*

E **Colocar** = *to put, place* (suggests a degree of precision)

El tendero colocó el florero en el centro del escaparate.	*The shopkeeper placed the vase in the middle of the window.*

Coloqué los libros en orden alfabético.   *I put the books in alphabetical order.*

F **Meter** = *to put (in)*
Metí la ropa en mi maleta.   *I put the clothes in my case.*
Voy a meter este dinero en el banco.   *I'm going to put this money in the bank.*

Meter la pata = *to put one's foot in it*
Julio siempre mete la pata.   *Julio always puts his foot in it.*

G **Apagar** = *to put out* (lights, etc.)
Apaguen las luces antes de salir.   *Switch off the lights before leaving.*

NB ¡No puedo más! ¡No puedo aguantarlo más! = *I can't put up with (it) any more!*

exercise

Translate the following into Spanish.

a Lay the table, Juanito.
b I can't put up with any more.
c She put on her new dress.
d They became sad.
e Julio put on the television.
f You always put your foot in it.
g I am going to put out the lights.
h They put the money in the bank.

The verb *tener* (to have) is used in a number of important expressions.

Tener *to have*: tengo, tienes, tiene, tenemos, tenéis, tienen

A The principal use of **tener** is to show possession.

Tenemos una casa en Madrid.	*We have a house in Madrid.*
No tengo tiempo para estudiar.	*I haven't got time to study.*

B **Tener que** followed by an infinitive indicates obligation.

Tengo que estudiar.	*I have to study.*
No tienes que trabajar hoy.	*You don't have to work today.*

C **Tener** is also used to form several idiomatic expressions.

- **tener frío / calor** = *to be cold/hot*

Tengo mucho frío / tengo mucho calor.	*I am very cold / hot.*

- **(no) tener razón** = *to be right (wrong)*

Usted no tiene razón.	*You are wrong.*

- **tengo hambre / sed** = *to be hungry / thirsty*

Tengo mucha hambre.	*I am very hungry.*
Julio tiene mucha sed.	*Julio is very thirsty.*

- **tener prisa** = *to be in a hurry*

Tengo (mucha) prisa.	*I am in a (great) hurry.*

- **tener cuidado** = *to be careful*

Tengo (mucho) cuidado.	*I am (very) careful.*

- **tener éxito** = *to be successful*

Tengo (mucho) éxito.	*I am (very) successful.*

- **tener miedo (de)** = *to be afraid (of)*
  Tengo (mucho) miedo de los osos.　　*I am (very) afraid of bears.*
- **(no) tener suerte** = *to be (un)lucky*
  Tengo (mucha) suerte en mis estudios.　　*I am (very) lucky in my studies.*
- **tener sueño** = *to be sleepy*
  Tengo (mucho) sueño.　　*I am (very) sleepy.*
- **tener ganas de** = *to feel like*
  Tengo (muchas) ganas de bailar. *I (really) feel like dancing.*
- **no tener nada que ver con** = *to have nothing to do with*
  Eso no tiene nada que ver con (Julio).　　*That's got nothing to do with (Julio) / It's none of (Julio's) business.*

There are many more expressions of this kind.

Remember, **tener** is a **pretérito grave**: tuve, tuviste … etc.

exercise

Reply to the following questions using an idiom with *tener*.

E.g. ¿Quieres una copa? → No, no tengo sed.

a ¿Quiere usted una hamburguesa?
b ¿Puedes venir al cine?
c ¿Por qué tomas un taxi?
d ¿Por qué lleva Julio tres jerseys y un poncho?
e ¿Has ganado la lotería?
f ¿Por qué no le hablas a Julio de tu problema?

Spanish uses different verbs for *to take* according to the context.

A In most contexts **tomar** can be used.

Voy a tomar esto.	*I'll take this (in a shop).*
Tome dos pastillas tres veces al día.	*Take two tablets three times a day.*
Tome la tercera calle a la derecha.	*Take the third street on the right.*

Tomar frequently translates *to have* with food or drink.

Vamos a tomar una copa.	*Let's have a drink.*
Tengo hambre: quiero tomar algo.	*I'm hungry: I want to eat something.*

Tomar can be used with transport.

Vamos a tomar el autobús.	*Let's get the bus.*

B **Coger** can also be used.

Cojo el autobús aquí.	*I catch the bus here.*

Coger usually means *to gather, pick (up), collect.*

A Luisa le gusta coger las flores.	*Luisa likes picking flowers.*
Coge tu sombrero y póntelo.	*Grab your hat and put it on.*
Cogí un resfriado.	*I caught a cold.*

NB Coger should be used with care in American Spanish – it frequently has obscene overtones. Use **tomar** instead.

C Llevar is used when taking people or animals somewhere.

Voy a llevar a mi novia a Acapulco.	*I'm taking my girlfriend to Acapulco.*
¿Adónde me lleva usted?	*Where are you taking me?*

Llevar also means to wear or to carry.

Mi amigo lleva un jersey rayado.	*My friend is wearing a striped jersey.*

D Sacar is used with the idea of *taking out*.

Quiero sacar cinco mil euros.	*I want to take out 5000 euro.*
Saqué este libro de la biblioteca.	*I got this book out of the library.*
Por Dios, sácame de aquí.	*For God's sake get me out of here.*
Vamos a sacar las entradas del cine con antelación.	*Let's get the cinema tickets in advance.*
Voy a sacar muchas fotos de la ciudad.	*I'm going to take lots of photos of the town.*

E With time, use **tardar en**.

Tardamos cinco horas en llegar.	*It took us five hours to get there.*

See exercise 40 in 'More practice'.

How to use *creer*, *pensar* and similar expressions.

A Creer = *to believe*

Creo en Dios.	*I believe in God.*
¿Crees tú en los fantasmas?	*Do you believe in ghosts?*
Creo que un día voy a ganar la lotería.	*I believe one day I shall win the lottery.*

It can also mean *to think*.

Creo que va a llover.	*I think it's going to rain.*

B Pensar que can also mean *to think*.

¿Piensas que va a llover?	*Do you think it's going to rain?*

Parece can be used in the same way

Parece que va a llover.	*It looks as if it's going to rain.*

Note the following idioms: **Creo que sí / Pienso que sí / Parece que sí** *I think so*; **Creo que no / Parece que no / Pienso que no** *I don't think so*.

C Pensar *to think* is used in different ways.

- **Pensar** plus an infinitive means *to intend*.

Mañana pienso madrugar.	*Tomorrow I intend to get up early.*

- **Pensar en** means *to have on one's mind, think about*.

Todo el tiempo Luisa piensa en Julio.	*Luisa thinks about Julio all the time.*

Pensamos en comprar un coche.	*We are thinking about buying a car.*

• **Pensar de** means *to have an opinion, think about.*

¿Qué piensas de este vestido?	*What do you think about this dress?*
¿Qué piensa Julio de tu coche nuevo?	*What does Julio think about your new car?*

NB If you make the verbs **creer** or **pensar** negative, you must use a subjunctive verb after **que** (see Unit 64).

No creo que Julio tenga el dinero.	*I don't think that Julio has the money.*

BUT

Creo que Julio no tiene el dinero.	*I think that Julio doesn't have the money.*

exercise

Complete the sentences with the expressions from the box.

a Julia _____ su novio.

b Mucha gente _____ los fantasmas.

c ¿Qué _____ mi coche nuevo?

d María y Pedro _____ casarse pronto.

e ¿Va a llover? ¿Qué te _____ ?

f Tú nunca _____ tu familia.

---

cree en   parece   piensa en   piensan   piensas de   piensas en

Spanish uses different verbs for *to try* according to the context. This unit summarizes the difference.

A Intentar = *to try, attempt*

Intentar is followed by a direct infinitive.

Siempre intenta ayudar.	*He always tries to help.*
Intentamos llegar al centro.	*We are trying to get to the centre.*

B Tratar = *to try, attempt*

Tratar needs **de** before an infinitive.

Luisa trata de recordar.	*Luisa tries to remember.*
Traté de encontrar la casa.	*I attempted to find the house.*

Tratar has another meaning: *to deal with, talk about.*

¿De qué trata la película?	*What is the film about?*
¿De qué se trata?	*What's it all about?*

C Probar = *to try, test, taste*

¿Quiere usted probar el vino?	*Do you want to try the wine?*
Probamos la paella pero no nos gustó.	*We tasted / tried the paella but we didn't like it.*
¡Es difícil pero vamos a probar!	*It's difficult but let's (give it a) try!*

D Probarse = *to try on* (clothes, shoes, etc.)

¿Son un cuarenta y tres? Quisiera probármelos.	*They're a size 43? I'd like to try them on.*

| Me probé los vaqueros en el probador. | *I tried on the jeans in the fitting room.* |

No me prueba = *It doesn't agree with me, suit me.*

| No me prueba el café. | *Coffee doesn't agree with me.* |

E **Ensayar** = *to try out, rehearse*

| Vamos a ensayar esta sinfonía. | *Let's run through this symphony.* |

F **Procesar** = *to try someone at law*

| Lo procesaron por haber robado el dinero. | *They tried him for stealing the money.* |

exercise

Put in the correct verb for to try (*intentar, tratar, probar, probarse, procesar*).

a Quiero _____ un plato típico.

b El hombre va a _____ de reparar el coche.

c Luisa siempre quiere _____ ayudar a la gente.

d Va a _____ los zapatos.

e Van a _____ al ladrón en agosto.

f Pensamos _____ el pescado.

g El niño no quiere _____ el traje nuevo.

h ¿Por qué no quieres _____ de ayudarnos?

i Los ladrones van a _____ de escaparse.

j Aquí se puede _____ el chocolate de la casa.

This unit explains how to say *for* in Spanish.

A The bad news is that Spanish has two common words for *for*: **para** and **por**. The good news is that they have a difference in meaning and avoid ambiguity.

¿Quiere usted darme gasolina para mi coche? Sí, ¿super o sin plomo?	*Would you give me petrol for my car? Yes, four star or unleaded?*
¿Quiere usted darme veinte litros de gasolina por mi coche? No, no vale tanto.	*Would you give me twenty litres of petrol for my car? No, it's not worth that much.*

In the first example, *for* means *to go into* and is translated by **para**; in the second example, *for* means *in exchange for* and is translated by **por**. This unit deals with **para**; see Unit 92 for the uses of **por**.

B **Para** = *for* (stresses destination, purpose, aim, achievement).

Salimos para Madrid.	*We are leaving for Madrid.*
Este regalo es para usted.	*This present is for you.*
Necesito una pieza para mi coche.	*I need a part for my car.*
Estudia para profesora.	*She's studying to be a teacher.*

C **Para** is used with an infinitive to mean *in order to*.

Trabajamos para comer.	*We work (in order) to eat.*

D **Para** tells when something is required.

Este ejercicio es para lunes.	*This exercise is for Monday.*

| ¿Tiene usted una habitación para esta noche? | *Do you have a room for tonight?* |

E **Para** is used with words like **siempre** and **entonces**.

| Adiós para siempre. | *Goodbye for ever.* |
| Para entonces el tren había salido. | *By that time the train had left.* |

F **Para** identifies a standard.

| Para médico no sabe mucho. | *For a doctor he doesn't know very much.* |

G **Para** also identifies someone's opinion.

| Para mí, la corrida es cruel. | *The bullfight is cruel, as far as I'm concerned.* |

exercise

Translate the following into Spanish.

a This present is for my father.
b The train is leaving for Barcelona.
c Is the wine for me?
d I need a part for my radio.
e Do you have two rooms for the night?
f I think the book is interesting.
g Luisa is studying to be a doctor.
h She only lives to study.
i For a singer he has a terrible voice.
j We are forever friends.

This unit contrasts the use of *por* with *para* (see Unit 91).

A Whereas **para** suggests aim or purpose, **por** stresses the reason or motivation behind an action.

Lo hizo por envidia.	*He did it for (= out of) spite.*
Gracias por el regalo.	*Thank you for the present.*
Te felicito por el resultado.	*I congratulate you for (= because of) the result.*
No pudimos salir por la lluvia.	*We couldn't go out for (= owing to) the rain.*
Lo hizo por su familia.	*He did it for (= for the sake of) his family.*
Se quejan por cualquier razón.	*They complain for any reason.*
¿Por qué no viniste?	*Why (= what for) didn't you come?*
Porque no tenía bastante dinero.	*Because I didn't have enough money.*
Fuimos al pueblo por pan.	*We went to the town for (= because we needed) bread.*

B **Por** is also used to express the means by which something is done.

Les mandé una carta por fax.	*I sent them a letter by fax.*
Tienes que ir por Madrid.	*You have to go by (= via) Madrid.*
No salgas por esas escaleras.	*Don't leave by those stairs.*

C Por suggests a vague location or time.

Por aquí no hay servicios públicos.	*There are no public toilets round here.*
La buscábamos por todas partes.	*We were looking for her everywhere.*
Trabajo por la tarde.	*I work in the afternoon.*

But **trabajo a las dos de la tarde** (*I work at 2 o'clock in the afternoon*) (precise time).

D Por is used for exchange or substitution.

Necesito dólares por estas libras esterlinas.	*I need dollars for these pounds.*
Pagué mil pesos por este traje.	*I paid a thousand pesos for this suit.*
Preparé la comida por mi madre.	*I prepared the meal for (= instead of) my mother.*

exercise

Use *por* to say who you did something for.

E.g. Preparé la comida (*for my mother*) → preparé la comida por mi madre.

a Lavé los platos (*for my mother*).

b Trabajamos en el jardín (*for my uncle*).

c Recogí las cartas (*for my neighbours*).

d Tomé la clase (*for the ill teacher*).

This unit tells you how to order coffee with or without sugar.

A **Con** = *with*

¿Quieres salir con Julio?	*Do you want to go out with Julio?*
Prefiero café con leche.	*I prefer coffee with milk.*
Una botella de agua con gas, por favor.	*A bottle of fizzy water, please.*

B **Con** is also used to say what you use.

Abrí la caja con una llave.	*I opened the box with a key.*
Tenemos que atarlo con cuerda.	*We must tie it with string.*

C **Con** may be used with an infinitive.

Con pulsar este botón, puede llamar a la criada.	*By pressing this button you can call the maid.*

D **Con** also expresses attitude or behaviour.

Ana era muy simpática con nosotros.	*Ana was very kind to us.*
Eres descortés conmigo.	*You are rude to me.*

Remember special personal pronouns **conmigo** *with me* and **contigo** *with you* (see Unit 27).

E **Con** is used with some expressions of clothing and appearance.

¡Qué guapa estás con esa falda!	*How pretty you look in that skirt!*

F Con also translates **a pesar de** *in spite of.*

Con tantas dificultades pudimos llegar a tiempo.

With (= in spite of) all the difficulties, we managed to arrive on time.

G Sin = *without*

Prefiero café sin azúcar. *I prefer coffee without sugar.*

agua sin gas *still mineral water*

gasolina sin plomo *unleaded petrol*

H After **sin**, the article is frequently omitted.

Quisiera una habitación sin ducha.

I'd like a room without a shower.

I Sin needs to be followed by a negative expression, such as **nada** *nothing*, **nadie** *no one* (see Unit 31).

Se fue sin nada. *He went away without anything.*

exercise

Put *con* or *sin* in the gaps to complete the sense.

a Soy vegetariano, necesito algo _____ carne.

b ¿Puede usted ayudarme? He salido _____ dinero.

c Prefiero té _____ limón porque me gusta la fruta.

d Café _____ azúcar, por favor. Tengo que guardar la línea.

e El estudiante salió _____ decir nada al profesor.

f No puedes ir _____ mí porque tengo las entradas.

g ¡No puedes abrir la botella _____ una cuchara!

h Para mí pescado _____ patatas. Muchas por favor.

A, de and *en* are three words which you will use over and over again to show directions, positions or movement.

A **En** shows where something or someone is and usually translates *in, on* or *at*. It is frequently used with the verb **estar**.

Madrid está en España.	*Madrid is in Spain.*
Mi madre está en casa.	*My mother is at home.*
El libro está en la mesa.	*The book is on the table.*

B If there is likely to be any ambiguity, use **sobre** to translate *on* and **dentro de** to emphasize *inside*.

El periódico está sobre la mesa.	*The newspaper is on the table.*
El pájaro está dentro de la casa.	*The bird is inside the house.*

C **A** expresses movement. It is used with verbs of motion like **ir** *to go*.

Vamos a Madrid, a España.	*Let's go to Madrid, to Spain.*
Mi madre va a casa.	*My mother is going home.*
Voy al trabajo.	*I'm going to work.*

Don't forget that **a** + **el** becomes **al**.

D A common exception is the verb **entrar** *to go in*. This is usually followed by **en** in Spain (though American Spanish prefers the more logical **a**).

Todos los días entro en la clase.	*Everyday I go into the classroom.*

E A is sometimes used to show position, when **en** would invite ambiguity.

Estamos sentados al sol.	*We're sitting in the sun (= shine).*

F Notice these expressions of transport: en (el) coche *by car*; en (el) autobús *by bus*; en (el) tren *by train*; en (el) avión *by plane*; a pie *on foot*; a caballo *riding, on horseback*.

A is also used after **llegar** *to arrive*.

El tren llega a la estación.	*The train arrives at the station.*

G A is used without a specific meaning but to indicate a direct object which is a specific person or people.

Quiero a Julio.	*I love Julio.*
Luisa nunca critica a los vecinos.	*Luisa never gossips about the neighbours.*

H De shows either origin, possession or movement from.

Es el coche de mi padre.	*It's my father's car.*
Salgo del trabajo a las seis.	*I leave work at six.*
He recibido una carta de mi amigo.	*I've received a letter from my friend.*

Remember that **de + el** becomes **del**.

See exercise 41 in 'More practice'.

This unit summarizes prepositions that show locations.

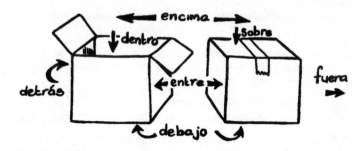

A Compound prepositions are followed by **de**: encima *over, above*; debajo *under, below*; detrás *behind*; delante *in front*; dentro *inside*; fuera *outside, away from*; cerca *near*; lejos *far from*; al lado *next to*; más allá *beyond*.

Encima de las casas los pájaros volaban.	*Birds were flying over the houses.*
Debajo de la tierra había minas.	*Under the ground there used to be mines.*
Dentro de la casa todo estaba tranquilo.	*Inside the house, all was quiet.*
Ahora vivimos fuera de la ciudad, lejos del centro.	*Now we live out of town, far from the centre.*

B These prepositions can be used as adverbs by dropping the **de**.

¿Dónde está Luisa? Dentro.   *Where is Luisa? Inside.*

C They can be intensified by adding **por**.

Había basura por dentro   *There was rubbish inside and*
y por fuera.   *out.*

D Simple prepositions include: entre *between*, en *in*, de *from*
and desde *from*.

Estaba sentada entre Juan   *She was sitting between Juan*
y Julio.   *and Julio.*

Hay un buen panorama   *There's a good view from the*
desde la ventana.   *window.*

NB These prepositions cannot be used as adverbs.

exercise

**This word puzzle uses prepositions. When you have completed
it, you will find another preposition in the shaded boxes.**

a Hay una farmacia cerca _____ mi casa.

b No hay cine _____ este pueblo.

c El hotel está _____ la panadería y el
restaurante.

d Hay algo duro _____ del paquete.

e Tenemos un jardín _____ de la casa.

f Hay un panorama magnífico _____
el balcón.

This unit looks at the different ways of expressing *before* in Spanish.

A **Antes de** = *before* (time)

Antes de is a compound preposition used with a noun or an infinitive in expressions of time.

antes de las nueve	*before nine o' clock*
antes de Navidad	*before Christmas*
Antes de salir vamos a comer.	*Let's eat before we go out.*

B With **antes de** + infinitive, the subject of the two parts of the expression should be the same: *We go out, we eat.*

If the subjects are not the same, **antes de** becomes a conjunction **antes (de) que** and requires a subjunctive verb (see Unit 64).

Tenemos que hacerlo antes (de) que venga Juan.	*We must do it before Juan comes.*

C **Ante** *before* is used in figurative expressions. It is not followed by **de**.

Ante todo, tenemos que trabajar.	*First of all we must work.*
¿Qué podemos hacer ante tantos problemas?	*What can we do faced with (= before) such problems?*
Julio compareció ante el juez.	*Julio came up before the judge.*

D **Delante de** = *before, in front of* (used for position)

Hay un parque delante de la plaza.	*There's a park in front of the square.*
Mi coche está delante de la casa.	*My car is in front of the house.*

E **Enfrente de** means *facing* or *opposite*.

La farmacia está enfrente del hotel.	*The chemist's is opposite the hotel.*
Hay que hacer cola enfrente del letrero.	*We must queue up in front of (= facing) the notice.*

Frente a can also be used for *facing*.

La parada está frente a nuestra casa.	*The (bus) stop is opposite our house.*

exercise

Put *ante*, *antes de*, *delante de*, *enfrente de* as appropriate in the gaps. Remember that *de* + *el* becomes *del*.

a Por favor, lava los platos _____ salir.

b Mira, la leche está _____ la cafetera.

c Creo que hay un hotel _____ el parque.

d Es difícil dormir bien _____ estos problemas.

e Paco tuvo que comparecer _____ el director porque no había estudiado bien.

97 miscellaneous prepositions

This unit summarizes a number of useful prepositions.

A Hasta = *until*

Vivimos aquí hasta septiembre.	*We are living here until September.*
Hasta la vista.	*Until we meet again, au revoir.*

B Desde = *since* (of time)

Vivimos aquí desde septiembre.	*We have been living here since September.*

Desde also means *from* (see Unit 95).

Hay una vista maravillosa desde la terraza.	*There's a wonderful view from the terrace.*

C Sobre = *about, concerning*

Es un libro sobre España.	*It's a book about Spain.*

D Hacia = *towards*

Caminaba hacia el pueblo.	*He was walking towards the town.*

E Según = *according to*

Según Julio, hay una fiesta mañana.	*According to Julio, there is a party tomorrow.*

F Durante = *during*

Trabajo durante las vacaciones.	*I work during the holidays.*

G Excepto, menos, salvo = *except*

Todos salieron, menos Luisa.	*They all left, except Luisa.*

H Debajo de *under* is a compound preposition referring to physical location.

Hay una moneda debajo de la mesa.	*There's a coin under the table.*

I Bajo is used for *under* in figurative contexts. It is not followed by **de**.

La vida bajo el dictador era difícil.	*Life under the dictator was difficult.*
bajo cero	*below zero*
El dinero estaba bajo llave.	*The money was under lock and key.*

J Detrás de *behind* is a compound preposition used to show position.

Hay un jardín detrás de la casa.	*There is a garden behind the house.*

K Tras means *behind*, *after* in figurative expressions.

día tras día, año tras año	*day after day, year after year*

L Después de is the usual compound preposition meaning *after*.

Estoy en casa después de las dos.	*I'm at home after two.*

See exercise 42 in 'More practice'.

Unit 2: a lámina b Dalí c Perú d Bogotá e límite
f café g fútbol h médico i feroces j francés
k posición l sigues m hizo n Paquita.

Unit 3: a el vino b la cerveza c la casa d el colegio
e el chico f la chica g el periódico h la revista i la
niña j el niño k la clase l la llave m el aceite
n la gente o el cine p el garaje q la madre r el té
s el café t el equipaje u la torre

Unit 4: a la luz b el arroz c la ciudad d la piel e el
cartel f el papel g el andaluz h la habitación i el
lápiz j la catedral • a una luz b un arroz c una
ciudad d una piel e un cartel f un papel g un
andaluz h una habitación i un lápiz j una catedral
• a las luces b los arroces c las ciudades d las pieles
e los carteles f los papeles g los andaluces h las
habitaciones i los lápices j las catedrales

Unit 5:

			¹F	
¹R	A	²D	I	O
		I	T	
		S	O	
		C		³M
⁴M	O	D	E	L	O
				O	
				T	
				O	

Unit 6: a una b un; la c una d una; un/el e el
f un g el h la; la i una/la j el

Unit 7: a el valor **b** el champú **c** el lunes **d** el rubí **e** el amor **f** la muchedumbre **g** la multitud **h** la crisis **i** la reunión **j** la serie **k** Cuba (feminine) **l** Australia (feminine) **m** China (feminine) **n** España (feminine)

Unit 8: a Spanish is pretty. **b** Teresa does not speak Spanish. **c** We live in India. **d** I don't like Mr Gómez. **e** Good morning, Mrs García.

Unit 9: a una naranja **b** un plátano **c** una manzana **d** un chico **e** una mesa **f** un coche **g** una luz **h** una ciudad **i** una habitación **j** un hospital **k** una aldea **l** una autora **m** una actriz **n** un ala

Unit 10: a dieciséis años **b** un euro **c** cuatro casas **d** nueve meses **e** diez chicas **f** un hombre **g** veintiocho días **h** veintiún hombres **i** un águila **j** dos cervezas

Unit 11: a Motor: mil novecientos ochenta y cuatro centímetros cuadrados **b** Potencia: ciento cincuenta caballos a seis mil revoluciones **c** Neumáticos: ciento noventa y cinco **d** Dimensiones exteriores: tres coma ochenta y cinco/uno coma sesenta y cuatro/uno coma cuarenta y un metros **e** Velocidad máxima: doscientos dieciséis kilómetros por hora **f** Aceleración cero a un kilómetro: treinta coma cuatro segundos **g** Consumo: nueve litros en cien kilómetros
h Precio: dieciocho mil euros

Unit 12: a veintidós de mayo   **b** dieciocho de enero
c cinco de agosto   **d** seis de marzo   **e** ocho de abril
f treinta de septiembre   **g** quince de febrero   **h** nueve de
diciembre

Unit 13: a Son las diez y veinte de la mañana.   **b** Son las
dos y cinco de la tarde.   **c** Son las nueve menos cuarto de la
mañana.   **d** Son las once y media de la mañana.   **e** Es la
una y pico de la tarde.   **f** Son las nueve menos algo de la
tarde.

Unit 14: a Enrique octavo   **b** Carlos quinto   **c** Juan
veintitrés   **d** Alfonso trece   **e** Juan Carlos primero
f el piso primero   **g** el piso tercero   **h** el siglo séptimo
i el piso once   **j** el siglo veinte

Unit 15: a hora   **b** tiempo   **c** hora   **d** tiempo   **e** veces
f vez   **g** veces   **h** tiempo

Unit 16: a una chica bonita   **b** las chicas bonitas   **c** La
casa es blanca.   **d** Las casas son blancas.   **e** Las mujeres
son inglesas.   **f** La revista es española.   **g** Ana es
trabajadora.   **h** Luisa y María son trabajadoras.   **i** Kylie
es australiana.   **j** Las chicas son españolas.

Unit 17: a Vivimos en una pequeña casa.   **b** Hay una
buena película en la televisión.   **c** Algún general vive aquí.
d Es un gran hombre.   **e** Es un hombre grande.   **f** Vivo
en Gran Bretaña.   **g** El pobre chico no tiene amigos.
h El hombre pobre no tiene dinero.   **i** El tercer libro/El

libro tercero no es bueno.   j El primer capítulo/El capítulo primero es malo.

Unit 18: a pequeño **b** bonito **c** muchas **d** viejas
e grandes **f** bonitos **g** amarillas **h** azules **i** azul
claro **j** raras **k** curiosos **l** diferente

Unit 19: a diferentemente **b** difícilmente **c** fácilmente
d formalmente **e** naturalmente **f** elegantemente
g mayormente **h** principalmente **i** inteligentemente
j cruelmente **k** evidentemente **l** responsablemente
m raramente **n** rápidamente **o** claramente
p estupendamente **q** lentamente **r** nerviosamente
s calmamente **t** tranquilamente **u** seriamente
v francamente **w** divinamente **x** furiosamente

Unit 21: a Barcelona es más grande que Sevilla pero menos
grande que Madrid.   **b** Carlos es más valiente que Federico
pero menos valiente que Juan.   **c** Luisa conduce más
rápidamente que mi hermana pero menos rápidamente que
Julia.   **d** Paco canta mejor que Miguel pero peor que Julio.

Unit 22: a Tengo el coche más viejo de la compañía.
b Tengo el peor asiento del teatro.   **c** Tengo la secretaria
menos trabajadora de la oficina.   **d** Tengo el colega más
hablador del departamento.   **e** Tengo la esposa más fea del
mundo.   **f** Tengo el dolor más terrible de todo.   **g** Tengo el
dentista menos simpático del pueblo.   **h** Tengo el día más
aburrido de la fábrica.   **i** Tengo las vacaciones menos largas
del colegio.   **j** Tengo el plato más asqueroso del restaurante.

Unit 23: a Aquellos chicos son inteligentes. **b** ¿Qué estudiantes son aquéllos? **c** ¿Qué es aquello? ¿Es carne? **d** Esta chica es muy bonita. **e** Ésta es mi hermana. **f** Aquellas montañas son bonitas. **g** ¿Qué montañas son aquéllas? **h** ¿Qué es esto? **i** ¿Qué chica es ésa? **j** ¿De quién es aquella falda?

Unit 24: a No, es mi coche. **b** No, es tu vino. **c** No, es su revista de ella. **d** No, son nuestras botas. **e** No, son sus periódicos de ellas.

Unit 26: a yo **b** nosotros **c** vosotros **d** ustedes **e** Ella; él **f** usted

Unit 28: a La tengo. **b** Los tengo. **c** Las tengo. **d** Lo tengo. **e** Lo tengo.

Unit 29: a Me lo dice. **b** Quiero hablarle/Le quiero hablar **c** No puedo decírtelo./No te lo puedo decir. **d** Te las entregamos. **e** Te lo doy. **f** Nos lo presenta.

Unit 30: a algo **b** alguien **c** Alguna **d** algo **e** alguna parte

Unit 31: a Tú nunca comes patatas. **b** Juan nunca llega tarde. **c** Nadie me ha ayudado en la casa. **d** Ningún español vive aquí. **e** Nada es interesante aquí. **f** Ninguna chica trabaja mucho.

Unit 33: a La chica que canta bien es la hermana de Luisa.
b El vino que se hace aquí no me gusta. **c** La fruta que se
vende en el mercado es mala. **d** El libro que me
recomendaste fue interesante. **e** El hotel en que nos
quedamos era muy caro.

Unit 34: a Qué **b** Quién **c** Qué **d** Quiénes **e** Qué
f Qué **g** Quién **h** Quiénes

Unit 35: a Cuáles/Qué **b** Qué **c** Dónde **d** Quiénes
e Cuánto **f** Cómo **g** Cuántos **h** Qué **i** Quién **j** Cuál

Unit 36: a e **b** y **c** y **d** e **e** y **f** y **g** u **h** o
i u **j** u **k** o

Unit 37: a pero **b** sino **c** pero **d** pero **e** sino **f** pero
g sino **h** sino **i** pero **j** sino

Unit 38: a bebe **b** Vivimos **c** Escribes **d** Fuman
e Charlo **f** Lee **g** Visitamos **h** Come

Unit 40: a ríe **b** cojo **c** escoge **d** conozco **e** huyen
f oye **g** envías **h** huele **i** continúan **j** prohíbe

Unit 41: a es **b** está **c** son **d** están **e** estás **f** eres

Unit 42: a soy; **b** estoy; **c** es; **d** es; **e** estoy;
f estoy; **g** están; **h** están; **i** está; **j** es; **k** son;
l es; **m** es; **n** está; **o** está

Unit 43: a estamos estudiando **b** estamos riendo **c** está muriendo **d** están robando **e** estoy aprendiendo **f** estáis saliendo **g** estás escribiendo **h** está esperando **i** estamos siguiendo **j** están repitiendo

Unit 44: a visto **b** sirve **c** hierve **d** pienso **e** tienen **f** sonríe **g** sigue **h** vienen **i** repiten **j** Dicen **k** quieren **l** cuentan **m** reímos **n** ríen **o** divierten **p** puedo **q** pierdo **r** sonrío **s** pido **t** vuelvo **u** siento **v** duermo **w** duerme **x** tiene

Unit 45: a Me levanto. **b** Me ducho. **c** Me visto. **d** Me acuesto.

Unit 46: a se para **b** para **c** pierdo **d** me pierdo **e** se cae **f** caen **g** detiene **h** se detiene **i** mover **j** moverse

Unit 47: a ¿Se puede pagar con dinero inglés? **b** ¿Se puede telefonear? **c** ¿Se puede comprar sellos? **d** ¿Se puede sacar fotos? **e** ¿Se puede cambiar dinero? **f** ¿Se puede usar una tarjeta de crédito? **g** ¿Se puede nadar? **h** ¿Se puede visitar la catedral?

Unit 48: a A María no le gusta el vino blanco. **b** A Julio y Julia les gusta el teatro. **c** (A mí) no me gusta trabajar. **d** A Julia le gusta salir con Julio. **e** ¿(A ti) te gusta la paella? **f** (A nosotros) no nos gustan las novelas.

Unit 50: a Es difícil alquilar un coche. **b** Está prohibido aparcar aquí. **c** Es más rápido ir en taxi. **d** Más vale ir al taller. **e** Es preferible comer temprano.

Unit 51: a saltó **b** abrimos **c** corrieron **d** cerré
e escuchasteis **f** nos sentamos **g** volvieron **h** sentiste
i contestaron

Unit 52: a pedí **b** sirvió **c** repetí **d** repitió **e** repetí
f pidió **g** siguió **h** sirvió **i** pedí

Unit 54: a Cantaba antes, pero ya no. **b** Éramos
estudiantes antes, pero ya no. **c** Nadaba Luisa antes, pero
ya no. **d** Practicabas deportes antes, pero ya no. **e** Iba de
paseo antes, pero ya no. **f** Escribían antes Julio e Isabel,
pero ya no. **g** Estudiábamos antes, pero ya no. **h**
Ustedes veían los partidos antes, pero ya no. **i** Ayudabais
antes, pero ya no. **j** Leía mucho antes, pero ya no.

Unit 55: a Hacía frío cuando Luisa compró la fruta.
b El sol brillaba cuando mi madre fue a la ciudad.
c Llovía cuando nosotros entramos. **d** Nevaba cuando mi
padre fue a trabajar. **e** Hacía viento cuando salí a nadar.
f Hacía sol cuando los estudiantes comenzaron a estudiar.

Unit 57: a Vamos a comer mucho. **b** Juan va a beber una
cerveza. **c** Luisa va a ir a la universidad. **d** Tú vas a
visitar América. **e** Vas a tener problemas. **f** Sí, pienso
lavar los platos. **g** Sí, pienso salir con Julio. **h** Sí, Juan
piensa comer toda la paella. **i** Sí, pienso pagar la cuenta.
j Sí, pienso servir la comida.

Unit 58: a No comería calamares. **b** No iría a pie.
c No vería la televisión. **d** No saldría con Luisa.
e No hablaría con el médico. **f** No trabajaría mucho.
g No diría la verdad. **h** No escribiría una carta. **i** No
podría llegar a tiempo. **j** No sabría la dirección.

Unit 59: a Han comido. **b** ¿Has terminado? **c** Han
creído. **d** Ha visto. **e** Hemos puesto. **f** Ha muerto.
g Habéis roto. **h** He descrito. **i** Han vuelto. **j** Ha
escrito.

Unit 60: a Pedro habrá terminado su libro. **b** Yo habré
pintado la casa. **c** Julio y Emilio se habrán casado. **d** Tú
y Julio habréis frito el pescado. **e** El pobre hombre habrá
muerto. **f** Tú y yo habremos recibido el dinero. **g** Usted
habrá hecho la paella. **h** Tú habrás escrito la carta. **i** Ellos
se habrán ido del pueblo. **j** Ustedes habrán visto la película.

Unit 61: *Suggested answers.* Tan pronto la policía había
llamado explicamos el problema. Como tú habías salido
me acosté. Cuando Carlos y María habían llegado salimos
juntos. Como nosotros habíamos terminado tomamos un
café.

Unit 62: a Yo no me habría acostado tarde. **b** Yo no los
habría fumado. **c** Yo no me habría casado. **d** Yo no
habría dormido toda la tarde. **e** Yo no lo habría estudiado.
f Yo no lo habría creído. **g** Yo no me habría bañado en el
mar. **h** Yo no la habría dicho. **i** Yo no me la habría
puesto. **j** Yo no me habría vuelto loco.

Unit 64: a trabajemos **b** griten **c** escriban **d** fumes
e cante **f** descanséis

Unit 65: a tenga **b** salgamos **c** vengas **d** diga
e hagamos **f** ponga **g** cuenten **h** nos divirtamos
i durmamos **j** veamos

Unit 66:

Unit 67: a Vamos a cantar/Cantaremos hasta que salgan los
niños. **b** Luisa va a descansar hasta que Julio venga/llegue.
c Compraré una casa grande cuando gane la lotería.
d Tan pronto como venga tu padre comeremos. **e** Estarán contentos cuando digas la verdad. **f** Vamos a
nadar hasta que empiece a llover.

Unit 68: a viene **b** tengo **c** tuviésemos **d** estuviera

Unit 69: a Es posible que llueva hoy. **b** Es probable que
no venga. **c** Puede ser que Pedro escriba pronto. **d** Es
dudoso que tengamos bastante dinero. **e** No es cierto que
podamos ir. **f** Quizá (etc.) llegue mañana. **g** Llegará
mañana, quizás. **h** Tal vez el hombre simpático pagará/
pague. **i** Quizás comprenda/entienda español. **j** A lo
mejor pronto te sientes mejor.

Unit 70: a hablas **b** gane **c** es **d** es **e** pidieses

Unit 71: a No se moleste. **b** No se lave. **c** No la abra.
d No la cierre. **e** No me diga. **f** No me pague. **g** No se
sienten. **h** No se lo ponga. **i** No se lo quiten.

Unit 72: a bebe, beded **b** habla, hablad **c** escribe,
escribid **d** vive, vivid **e** corre, corred **f** levántate,
levantaos **g** acuéstate, acostaos **h** vístete, vestíos
i duérmete, dormíos **j** escóndete, escondeos

Unit 73: a que Luisa comiese/comiera. **b** que los niños
trabajasen/trabajaran. **c** que el estudiante entrase/entrara.
d que el profesor saliese/saliera. **e** que usted no
fumase/fumara. **f** que Julio llegase/llegara. **g** que
cantase/cantara. **h** que no bebieseis/bebierais.

Unit 74: a Quiere comer. **b** Prefiero descansar. **c** Deciden
comprar. **d** No puedes salir hoy. **e** Debemos estudiar.
f Olvidan escribir. **g** ¿Piensas ir?

Unit 75: a Vamos a tocar el piano. **b** Salgo a pasear en el
parque. **c** Comienza a leer. **d** Empezamos a escribir.
e Luisa aprende a nadar. **f** Julio estudia a ser mecánico.
g Nos obliga a descansar. **h** Te invitamos a comer.

Unit 76: a se encargó **b** se acordó **c** me arrepentí
d trato **e** se jactaron **f** presume **g** he dejado **h** Me
he olvidado

Unit 77: a en **b** por **c** por **d** en **e** con **f** en **g** en
h con

Unit 79: a Yo acabo de comer pero vuelvo a comer en
seguida. **b** Usted acaba de nadar pero vuelve a nadar en
seguida. **c** Julio acaba de cantar pero vuelve a cantar en
seguida. **d** Nosotros acabamos de leer pero volvemos a leer
en seguida. **e** Ellos acaban de jugar al tenis pero vuelven a
jugar al tenis en seguida. **f** Tú acabas de salir pero vuelves
a salir en seguida. **g** Los señores García acaban de llamar
pero vuelven a llamar en seguida. **h** Tú acabas de hacer
una paella pero vuelves a hacer una paella en seguida. **i**
Nosotros acabamos de ir a la ciudad pero volvemos a ir a la
ciudad en seguida. **j** Ustedes acaban de escribir pero
vuelven a escribir en seguida.

Unit 80: a conoce **b** sabe **c** conoce **d** conozco
e sé **f** conoces

Unit 81: a Puede **b** puedo **c** puedes **d** sé **e** puede
f puedo **g** sé **h** sabe; puede; puede

Unit 82: a Siempre se pone pálida. **b** Quieren hacerse
ricos. **c** Los estudiantes llegaron a ser/se hicieron
profesores. **d** Mi profesor se volvió loco. **e** No quiero
engordar. **f** Me canso rápidamente. **g** Pedro se enoja
rápidamente. **h** Es fácil emocionarse. **i** Nunca nos
haremos amigos/No nos haremos amigos nunca. **j** Se han
vuelto imposibles.

Unit 83: *Possible versions.* Julio a veces deja las llaves en casa. Julio mañana se marcha/se va de la oficina/de Granada. El tren siempre/a veces sale tarde. El trabajo nunca sale bien. Julio mañana abandona a su familia/Barcelona.

Unit 84: a miramos **b** parece **c** busca **d** Ojo **e** cuidado **f** repasar

Unit 85: a Te echo de menos **b** faltaba **c** perdí **d** Me **e** erró **f** No

Unit 86: a Pon la mesa, Juanito. **b** No puedo más./No puedo aguantarlo más. **c** Se puso el vestido nuevo. **d** Se pusieron tristes. **e** Julio puso la televisión. **f** Siempre metes la pata. **g** Voy a apagar las luces. **h** Metieron el dinero en el banco.

Unit 87: a *Suggested answers.* **a** Sí/no, (no) tengo (mucha) hambre. **b** No, no tengo tiempo./No, no tengo ganas. **c** Porque tengo (mucha) prisa. **d** Porque tiene (mucho) frío. **e** Sí/No, (no) tengo (mucha) suerte. **f** Mi problema no tiene nada que ver con Julio.

Unit 89: a piensa en **b** cree en **c** piensas de **d** piensan
e parece **f** piensas en

Unit 90: a probar **b** tratar **c** intentar **d** probarse
e procesar **f** probar **g** probarse **h** tratar **i** tratar
j probar.

Unit 91: a Este regalo es para mi padre. **b** El tren sale
para Barcelona. **c** ¿Es el vino para mí? **d** Necesito una
pieza para mi radio. **e** ¿Tiene dos habitaciones para la
noche? **f** Para mí, el libro es interesante. **g** Luisa estudia
para médico. **h** Sólo vive para estudiar. **i** Para cantante
tiene una voz terrible. **j** Somos amigos para siempre.

Unit 92: a por mi madre **b** por mi tío **c** por mis vecinos
d por el profesor enfermo

Unit 93: a sin **b** sin **c** con **d** sin **e** sin **f** sin
g con **h** con

Unit 95:

Unit 96: a antes de **b** delante de **c** enfrente del **d** ante
e ante

Exercise 1 (Unit 2)

Write down the Spanish for these words, paying attention to the need for an accent.

a yes
b if
c my
d me

e you
f your
g like
h how

Exercise 2 (Unit 4)

Give the singular of the following nouns.

Eg los chicos → el chico

a las casas
b los lápices
c las ciudades
d los carteles
e las universidades

f los papeles
g las luces
h las habitaciones
i los andaluces
j las pieles

Exercise 3 (Unit 5)

Give the Spanish for the following.

a I have (**Tengo**) a good radio.
b The photo of the children is fantastic.
c Julio's motorbike is fast (**rápida**).
d María is a beautiful model.
e the house on the right

f the door (**la puerta**) on the left
g We are going (**Vamos**) to the disco.
h There are (**Hay**) many (**muchas**) discos here (**aquí**).
i I have a second-hand car.
j Give me your hands.

Exercise 4 (Unit 8)

Put in the definite article if it is required.

E.g. ¿Tiene usted _____ hijos? → ¿Tiene usted hijos?

a No me gustan _____ tomates.
b _____ pan francés es muy bueno.
c ¿Te gusta _____ vino?
d No bebo _____ vino.
e ¿Hay _____ pan?
f _____ español es difícil.
g _____ agua por favor.
h ¿Dónde vive _____ señor López?
i ¿Qué quieres, _____ vino o _____ café?
j _____ España es diferente.
k _____ España de los turistas es diferente.

Exercise 5 (Unit 10)

Put the numbers into words. Make sure you use the correct form *un*, *-ún* or *una* with these expressions!

a 21 euros

b 121 libros

c 131 casas

d 51 hombres

e 81 revistas

f 101 chicas

g 31 niños

h 161 cigarrillos

i 191 botellas

j 71 estudiantes

Exercise 6 (Unit 11)

Write these years in full.

a 1066

b 1215

c 1492

d 1588

e 1789

f 1898

g 1936

h 1945

i 2000

j 2003

Exercise 7 (Unit 12)

Which month is being referred to?

a A principios del año, tiene treinta y un días.

b El mes antes de junio con treinta y un días.

c El mes a mediados del año con treinta días.

d Este mes tiene un día más algunos años.

e En primavera; tiene treinta días.

f En otoño, con treinta días.

g A fines del año; tiene treinta y un días.

h Entre julio y septiembre, en verano.

Exercise 8 (Unit 13)

Translate the following into Spanish.

a The train leaves (**sale**) at ten a.m.
b The film (**La película**) begins (**empieza**) at five on the dot.
c Julio is coming (**viene**) at half past nine.
d It's gone six!
e My watch is slow.
f I am going out (**Voy a salir**) just before ten.
g Silence (**Silencio**) – it's five in the morning.
h Is your watch fast?
i It's a quarter to four.
j It's just gone three.

Exercise 9 (Unit 16)

Make these expressions plural.

E.g. la chica francesa → las chicas francesas

a el chico italiano
b la casa azul
c la revista inglesa
d el actor americano
e la chica trabajadora
f la esposa mandona
g la falda gris
h la bota marrón
i el hombre diferente
j la chica triste

Exercise 10 (Unit 18)

Make the adjective agree as necessary.

E.g. una casa (blanco y negro) → una casa blanca y negra
una casa y un jardín (grande) → una casa y un jardín grandes

a casa (pequeño/blanco)

b (mucho) niños y niñas

c faldas y blusas (amarillo)

d chicas y profesoras (bonito)

e chicas y chicos (trabajador)

f periódicos y revistas (alemán)

g revistas y películas (español)

h un general (gran/importante)

i un general (grande/importante)

j un libro (buen/inglés)

Exercise 11 (Unit 19)

You are describing how someone reacted to a recent incident. Complete the sentences with the appropriate adverbs.

E.g. Juan estaba furioso – gritó _____ . → Juan estaba furioso – gritó furiosamente.

a Luisa es una persona sincera – explicó todo _____ .

b Julio es un buen conductor – condujo _____ .

c El profesor es muy inteligente – describió la situación

_____ .

d Normalmente la policía es puntual – llegó _____ .

e Rodrigo tiene un carácter malo – actuó _____ .

f El incidente fue muy rápido – todo ocurrió _____ .

g El inspector es un hombre serio – habló _____ .

h Soy una persona sincera – lo digo _____ .

i Tú eres un conductor cuidadoso – viaja _____ .

j Es fácil comprender la situación – comprendiste _____ .

Exercise 12 (Unit 20)

Fill the blanks with *que, de, de lo que, del que, de la que, de los que, de las que*, as necessary.

a El coche cuesta menos _____ un millón de pesetas.

b Un coche cuesta más _____ una moto.

c Un coche cuesta menos _____ dice mi padre.

d Mi coche usa menos gasolina _____ piensas.

e Mi coche usa menos aceite _____ gasolina.

f En Madrid hay más parques _____ dice este libro.

g Tú necesitas menos camisas _____ tienes.

h El billete cuesta más dinero _____ tengo.

i Voy al cine más frecuentemente _____ tú.

j Julia tiene más _____ veinte pares de zapatos.

Exercise 13 (Unit 22)

Practise absolute superlatives using *-ísimo*. Pick adjectives from the box.

E.g ¿Qué tal el chocolate? → Es sabrosísimo. (*How's the chocolate? It's really tasty.*)

¿Qué tal...

a el vino? b el coche? c la casa? d el traje? e la playa? f las patatas? g los caramelos? h los ejercicios? i las chicas? j las discos?

> elegante cómodo sabroso dulce bueno fácil
> guapo vivo rico rápido

Exercise 14 (Unit 25)

Play a game of one-upmanship.

E.g. Tu casa es grande. → Tu casa es grande, pero la mía es más grande.

a Tu coche es rápido.

b Tu familia es inteligente.

c Tus padres son trabajadores.

d Tus hermanas son estúpidas.

e Tu trabajo es difícil.

f Tu habitación es bonita.

g Tu amiga es hermosa.

h Tus botas son elegantes.

i Tu colegio es famoso.

j Tus tías son ricas.

Exercise 15 (Unit 27)

Complete the sentences with the appropriate pronoun.

E.g. Hoy es mi cumpleaños – ¿tienes un regalo para _____ ?
→ ¿tienes un regalo para mí?

a Hoy es tu cumpleaños – tengo un regalo para _____ .

b Hoy es el cumpleaños de Juan – tengo un regalo para _____ .

c Hoy es su cumpleaños, don José – tengo un regalo para

_____ .

d Hoy es su aniversario, señores – tengo un regalo para

_____ .

e Hoy es nuestro aniversario – ¿tenéis un regalo para _____ ?

f Claro, mamá y papá – tenemos un regalo para _____ .

g Niñas, tengo limonada para _____ .

h Mi hermana y yo estamos enfermas – ¿tiene usted medicina para _____ ?

Exercise 16 (Unit 28)

Practise the order of object pronouns.

E.g. (el café) (beber) he bebido → No lo he bebido, voy a beberlo.

a (la cerveza) (beber) he bebido

b (la casa) (limpiar) he limpiado

c (yo) (ducharse) he duchado

d (el coche) (conducir) he conducido

e (los niños) (ver) he visto

f (las botellas) (lavar) he lavado

Exercise 17 (Unit 32)

Supply a suitable response from the box.

a ¿Qué quieres hacer?

b ¿Cuándo piensas ir a una corrida (*bullfight*)?

c ¿Quieres ir a la corrida?

d ¿No quieres ir al restaurante?

e ¿Qué zapatos prefieres?

f ¿Quién canta?

g ¿Qué has dicho?

h ¿Has comido algo tan malo?

i ¿Has decidido?

j No has comido la carne, ¿no vas a comer el pescado?

nunca	nada	nadie	en la vida	en absoluto
tampoco	todavía no	ya no	ningunos	nada

Exercise 18 (Unit 33)

Fill the gaps with the appropriate form of *el cual, la cual, los cuales, las cuales*.

E.g. La casa en _____ vivo es muy vieja. → La casa en la cual vivo es muy vieja.

a El mar debajo de _____ hay petróleo es muy profundo.

b La plaza cerca de _____ vives es muy grande.

c Aquí ves la iglesia enfrente de _____ está el bar.

d Los coches con _____ trabaja el mecánico son viejos.

e Abrió el armario en _____ guardaba la comida.

f Éstas son las llaves sin _____ salieron.

Exercise 19 (Unit 38)

Give the required forms of the following basic verbs.

E.g. *I* (hablar) → hablo

a *we* (hablar)

b *we* (comer)

c *we* (vivir)

d *you* (*familiar singular*) (comer)

e *he* (vivir)

f *they* (comer)

g *you* (*polite singular*) (hablar)

h *I* (comer)

i *you* (*familiar plural*) (vivir)

j *you* (*polite plural*) (hablar).

Exercise 20 (Unit 39)

Give the first person singular and plural (*I* and *we* forms) of the following verbs.

a salir

b poner

c hacer

d traer

e caer

f dar

g ir

h saber

i conducir

j conocer

Exercise 21 (Unit 41)

Put in the correct form of the present tense of *ser*.

E.g. Nosotros _____ mecánicos. → Nosotros somos mecánicos.

a Tú _____ estudiante.

b Juan _____ mecánico.

c Julio y Pedro _____ amigos.

d Yo _____ turista.

e Madrid _____ la capital de España.

f Vosotros _____ ingleses.

g Hoy _____ lunes.

h _____ las dos.

i Hoy _____ el dos de mayo.

j Usted _____ profesor.

Exercise 22 (Unit 41)

Put in the correct form of the present tense of *estar*.

E.g. Londres _____ en Inglaterra. → Londres está en Inglaterra.

a Los estudiantes _____ en la clase.

b ¿Dónde _____ Julio?

c Juan y Pedro _____ en la ciudad.

d ¿Dónde _____ los servicios?

e El hotel _____ en la plaza Mayor.

f Nosotros _____ en casa.

g ¿_____ María? No, no _____ aquí.

h ¿Vosotros _____ en Madrid?

i Yo _____ en el café.

j Ustedes no _____ en el centro de la ciudad.

Exercise 23 (Unit 44)

Fill in the missing forms of the radical-changing verbs.

a **decir** *to say:* digo, dices, dice, decimos, decís, _____ .

b **fregar** *to scrub:* friego, _____ , friega, fregamos, fregáis, friegan.

c **perder** *to lose:* _____ , pierdes, pierde, perdemos, perdéis, pierden.

d **volver** *to return:* _____ , _____ , _____ , volvemos, volvéis, _____ .

e **reír** *to laugh:* río, _____ , _____ , reímos, reís, _____ .

Exercise 24 (Unit 49)

Complete the sentences with an appropriate expression from the box.

a ¡Ay! Me _____ el diente.

b ¿Dónde hay una farmacia? Me _____ comprar aspirinas.

c No te _____ aspirinas. Te _____ dos en este paquete.

d Voy al partido esta noche porque me _____ el Real Madrid.

e Me _____ la ópera.

f Si no quieres ir al cine, voy solo. No me _____ .

g A ti te _____ lavar los platos.

h Julio quiere comprar el periódico pero le _____ un peso.

i Sí, mañana me _____ .

j Te _____ bien la falda. Es muy elegante.

> chifla   conviene   duele   encanta   falta   hace falta
> hacen falta   importa   quedan   sienta   toca

Exercise 25 (Unit 51)

Fill the gaps with appropriate verb from the box to make a logical sequence.

Anoche me a _____ temprano. Me b _____ en seguida pero, después de una hora, c _____ un ruido terrible y me d _____ . Me e _____ en la cama y f _____ . ¿Qué es?, g _____ pero nadie h _____ . De repente i _____ pasos detrás de la puerta. ¿Quién es?, j _____ a gritar, y k _____ a temblar de miedo. Luego algo, o alguien, l _____ a la puerta. m _____ de la cama y n _____ a la puerta. La o _____ pero no p _____ nada al principio. ¿Quién es?, q _____ en voz baja. Luego, en el pasillo algo se r _____ Una figura oscura se me s _____ . No la t _____ , pero u _____ a una persona vieja, delgada y melancólica. v _____ la puerta y w _____ llamar a la policía.

> abrí   acercó   acosté   cerré   contestó   corrí   decidí   descubrí
> desperté   dormí   empecé   escuché   fue   grité   llamó   movió
> oí   reconocí   repetí   salté   senté   sentí   vi   volví

Exercise 26 (Unit 53)

Translate the verbs to say what Julio and Julia got up to yesterday.

Ayer, Julia (**a** *wanted*) salir con Julio. Julia (**b** *said*) 'Hay una película buena en el cine que (**c** *produced*) un director famoso'. Julio no le (**d** *made*) caso (*pay attention*). Julia (**e** *put*) un billete de banco en la mesa. 'Ahora podemos ir', (**f** *he replied**) '. '¿A qué hora termina la película?' (**g** *said*) los niños. '(**h** *I said*) que (**i** *I put*) las horas de las sesiones en tu bolso', (**j** *said*) uno de los niños. Entonces Julia (**k** *knew*) lo que (**l** *did*) los niños, y por fin Julia (**m** *was able*) encontrar el horario. Julia y Julio (**n** *drove*) a la ciudad y pronto (**o** *came*) al cine. Todos (**p** *had*) buena suerte porque la película, el viaje y los buenos actores (**q** *put*) un buen fin al día.

*to reply **reponer**

Exercise 27 (Unit 54)

Complete this story, inserting the appropriate verb forms for the imperfect.

Cuando nosotros (**a** ser) niños, (**b** vivir) en un pueblo pequeño. Nuestros abuelos (**c** vivir) en el mismo pueblo. Mi padre (**d** ser) mecánico en la ciudad y mi madre (**e** trabajar) por la mañana también. Cuando ella (**f** volver) a casa, (**g** comer) todos juntos y después mis hermanos y yo (**h** jugar) en el parque. Todos los días mi padre (**i** ir) a su trabajo muy temprano y cuando (**j** entrar) en la casa (**k** estar) muy cansado. Mi padre (**l** beber) algo, (**m** ver) la televisión y (**n** dormir) un poco. Nosotros (**o** pasar) las tardes en casa y a las diez todos nos (**p** acostar) y (**q** esperar) otro día.

Exercise 28 (Unit 55)

Complete the story with the preterite or imperfect of the verbs as necessary.

El otro día (**a** hacer) sol, así nosotros (**b** decidir) salir al campo. (**c** Hacer) un poco frío y nos (**d** poner) el abrigo y los guantes. Luisa no (**e** querer) venir pero por fin la (**f** persuadir) su novio, que también (**g** venir) con nosotros. Nosotros no (**h** coger) paraguas porque no (**i** llover) cuando (**j** salir). (**k** Ser) las once en punto. Después de media hora (**l** llegar) a un bosque y (**m** entrar). (**n** Ser) muy tranquilo porque nadie (**o** estar) allí. De repente Juan (**p** oír) algo raro. (**q** Ser) el ruido de una tormenta. Inmediatamente (**r** empezar) a llover y (**s** tener) que volver corriendo a casa. Cuando (**t** llegar), (**u** estar) completamente calados (*drenched*) por la lluvia. Pero, ¡qué sorpresa! La puerta (**v** estar) abierta. Alguien se (**w** mover) en la casa. ¿Quién (**x** poder) ser? ...

Exercise 29 (Unit 56)

Say that the person will do something tomorrow, using the future tense.

E.g. No bebo el vino hoy. → Beberé el vino mañana.

a No pago la cuenta hoy (*pay the bill*).

b Luisa no contesta a la carta (*answer the letter*).

c Julio y Pedro no reparan el coche (*repair the car*).

d No vemos la película (*see the film*).

e Tú no vuelves a casa (*go back home*).

f Usted no escribe la carta (*write the letter*).

g Emilio no va a la ciudad (*go to town*).

h No dormimos aquí (*sleep here*).

i No me levanto temprano (*get up early*).

j Vosotros no os bañáis en el mar (*bathe in the sea*).

Exercise 30 (Unit 63)

The following sentences sound rather inelegant and unnatural in Spanish. Change the passive into the construction with *se*.

E.g. Este pan es vendido en todas las tiendas. → Se vende este pan en todas las tiendas.

a La paella es comida por toda España.

b El inglés es hablado en muchos países.

c Muchos cigarrillos son fumados en la calle.

d El vino tinto es bebido con frecuencia.

e Las cartas son escritas con lápiz.

f La puerta es abierta lentamente.

g Este periódico es leído mucho.

h La hierba es comida en el verano.

i Las flores son cogidas en el campo.

j El pueblo es conocido.

Exercise 31 (Unit 64)

Give the correct form of the present subjunctive.

E.g. ¿Julio quiere trabajar? (nosotros) → Julio quiere que nosotros trabajemos.

a ¿Julio prefiere descansar? (nosotros)

b ¿Julio espera ganar la lotería? (Luisa)

c ¿Julio quiere comer? (usted)

d ¿Julio necesita contestar? (Juan y María)

e ¿Julio no quiere fumar? (tú)

f ¿Julio quiere lavarse? (los niños)

g ¿Julio necesita trabajar? (vosotros)

h ¿Julio no quiere gritar? (la gente)

i ¿Julio no quiere escribir? (yo)

j ¿Julio insiste en beber? (las chicas)

Exercise 32 (Unit 65)

Fit the subjunctives in the grid. The clues are not necessarily in order!

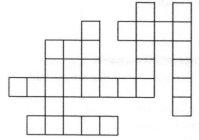

a Espero que el niño no
  (caer).
b Mi madre prefiere que
  Juan no (ver) la película.
c Espero que María y yo
  (tener) bastante dinero.
d Quiero que mi madre
  (hacer) una paella.
e Insisto en que tú (pedir)
  permiso.
f Luisa quiere que Julio
  (decir) la verdad.
g El profesor prohíbe que
  los niños (salir).
h Esperamos que Ana
  (viene).

Exercise 33 (Unit 68)

Use an imperfect subjunctive after *si*.

E.g. ser rico → Si fuese/fuera rico compraría un coche.
a tener dinero
b vivir en el campo

c saber conducir
d ver bien
e visitar a mis amigos
f beber menos

Exercise 34 (Unit 70)

Use *ojalá* and an imperfect subjunctive.

E.g. No hablo español. → Ojalá hablase/hablara español.

a No tengo dinero.
b Julio no me visita.
c Elena no me escribe.
d Mis padres no son ricos.
e No hablas español.

Exercise 35 (Unit 71)

Rewrite the infinitives of these instructions using the *ustedes* (polite plural) commands.

E.g. Cortar el papel. → Corten el papel.
Beber más leche. → Beban más leche.

a Abrir el paquete.
b Llenar el depósito con aqua.
c No aparcar.
d Pagar la cuenta al salir.
e No pisar la hierba.
f No cantar en el bar.

Exercise 36 (Unit 73)

Give the alternative form for the imperfect subjunctive.

E.g. hablases → hablaras
comiéramos → comiésemos

a hablases
b comieras
c fuera
d fuésemos
e saliera

f bebiesen
g hablarais
h dijese
i hicieses
j bebieras

Exercise 37 (Unit 78)

Use *haber* in the appropriate tense to translate *there is/has been/will be*, etc.

E.g. There had been a bullfight. → Había habido una corrida.

a There used to be lots of donkeys on the beach.
b There has been an accident.
c There is going to be a bullfight.
d There will be many candidates for the job.
e Without money there would be a strike.
f There had been a car in the garage.
g Suddenly there was a knock on the door.
h There aren't any toilets in the bar.

Exercise 38 (Unit 80)

This puzzle revises *saber*, *conocer* and *poder* (from Unit 81). The ten missing verbs are in the word grid. Three are upside down.

S	P	O	C	O	S	A
C	O	N	O	C	E	S
O	D	E	N	O	D	A
N	E	B	O	N	E	B
O	M	A	C	O	U	E
C	O	S	E	C	P	I
E	S	A	B	E	I	S

a Nosotros _____ salir esta tarde.

b ¿Tú _____ a María?

c Pedro no _____ Granada.

d Vosotros _____ hablar español.

e Usted _____ Madrid.

f Luisa no _____ a Julio.

g Tú no _____ ir al cine.

h Yo _____ tocar la guitarra bien.

i María y Luisa no _____ que Julio está aquí.

j Vosotros no _____ nada de mi trabajo.

Exercise 39 (Unit 86)

Fill the gaps with the appropriate infinitive: *poner, ponerse, meter, colocar, aguantar* or *apagar*.

E.g. Voy a _____ el dinero en este cajón. → Voy a meter el dinero en este cajón.

a Luisa quiere _____ su vestido nuevo.

b Creo que Julio va a _____ la pata otra vez.

c El camarero fue a _____ el florero en la mesa.

d ¡La película es terrible! No la puedo _____ más.

e ¿Queréis _____ la mesa para comer, niños?

f Prefiere no _____ todo su dinero en el banco.

g Vamos a _____ los sellos en este álbum.

h Voy a _____ la luz porque el sol brilla.

i Juan quiere _____ la radio para oír el programa.

j Pedro no va a _____ el traje gris.

Exercise 40 (Unit 88)

Complete this account with the correct form of *to take* from the box.

Cuando voy a la ciudad, normalmente a _____ el autobús, pero esta mañana b _____ un taxi porque estaba lloviendo. También tuve que c _____ a los niños porque hoy no hay colegio. En la ciudad entramos en la biblioteca y d _____ libros. Luego vistamos el banco donde e _____ dinero. En la cafetería f _____ café o limonada. Después, en el parque, g _____ fotos de las flores, pero, claro, ¡no las h _____ ! A las tres i _____ el autobús a casa, pero j _____ mucho tiempo en llegar. Una vez en casa, k _____ la botella de aspirinas del armario y l _____ dos pastillas.

---

cogimos   cogimos   cojo   llevar   sacamos   sacamos
sacamos   saqué   tardamos   tomamos   tomé   tomé

Exercise 41 (Unit 94)

Decipher this message by putting in the missing *a*, *al*, *de*, *del* or *en*.

Julio, estoy a _____ la ciudad. Quiero ir b _____ mercado que está c _____ el centro cerca d _____ la plaza mayor. No puedo volver e _____ el autobús porque tengo que estar f _____ la casa g _____ mi amiga h _____ las cinco i _____ la tarde. Queremos sentarnos j _____ el balcón para criticar a los vecinos que están k _____ la costa l _____ vacaciones. Pero nosotras preferimos estar m _____ la sombra. ¿Quieres venir n _____ la ciudad o _____ tu coche para llevarme p _____ mercado q _____ la casa r _____ Luisa? No quiero ir s _____ pie. Gracias. Besos, Julia.

Exercise 42 (Unit 97)

Complete the sentences with the appropriate preposition.

a Vamos a continuar aquí _____ octubre.
b Viven en Málaga _____ el año pasado.
c Hay una vista magnífica _____ nuestro balcón.
d Su actitud _____ su mujer es algo rara.
e Caminamos lentamente _____ el río.
f Todos _____ Julio jugaban al fútbol.
g Tengo que estudiar _____ la semana.
h _____ Pedro, hay una película buena hoy.
i ¿Tiene usted un libro _____ la cocina española?
j Por favor, no hablen _____ la película.

Exercise 1 (Unit 2): a sí b si c mi d mí e tú f tu g como h cómo

Exercise 2 (Unit 4): a la casa b el lápiz c la ciudad d el cartel e la universidad f el papel g la luz h la habitación i el andaluz j la piel

Exercise 3 (Unit 5): a Tengo una radio buena. b La foto de los niños es fantástica. c La moto de Julio es rápida. d María es una modelo hermosa. e la casa a la derecha. f la puerta a la izquierda. g Vamos a la disco. h Hay muchas discos aquí. i Tengo un coche de segunda mano. j Dame las manos.

Exercise 4 (Unit 8): a a No me gustan los tomates. b El pan francés es muy bueno. c ¿Te gusta el vino? d No bebo vino. e ¿Hay pan? f El español es difícil. g Agua, por favor. h ¿Dónde vive el señor López? i ¿Qué quieres, vino o café? j España es diferente. k La España de los turistas es diferente.

Exercise 5 (Unit 10): a veintiún euros b ciento veintiún libros c ciento treinta y una casas d cincuenta y un hombres e ochenta y una revistas f ciento una chicas g treinta y un niños h ciento sesenta y un cigarrillos i ciento noventa y una botellas j setenta y un estudiantes

Exercise 6 (Unit 11): a mil sesenta y seis b mil doscientos quince c mil cuatrocientos noventa y dos d mil quinientos ochenta y ocho e mil setecientos ochenta y nueve f mil ochocientos noventa y ocho   g mil novecientos treinta y seis   h mil novecientos cuarenta y cinco   i dos mil   j dos mil tres

Exercise 7 (Unit 12): a enero   b mayo   c junio   d febrero   e abril   f noviembre   g diciembre   h agosto

Exercise 8 (Unit 13): a El tren sale a las diez de la mañana. b La película empieza a las cinco en punto.   c Julio viene a las nueve y media.   d Son las seis pasadas.   e Mi reloj está atrasado.   f Voy a salir a las diez menos algo. g Silencio – son las cinco de la madrugada.   h ¿Tu reloj está adelantado?   i Son las cuatro menos cuarto.   j Son las tres y pico.

Exercise 9 (Unit 16): a los chicos italianos   b las casas azules   c las revistas inglesas   d los actores americanos e las chicas trabajadoras   f las esposas mandonas   g las faldas grises   h las botas marrones   i los hombres diferentes   j las chicas tristes

Exercise 10 (Unit 18): a una pequeña casa blanca. b muchos niños y niñas.   c faldas y blusas amarillas. d chicas y profesoras bonitas.   e chicas y chicos trabajadores.   f periódicos y revistas alemanes.   g revistas y películas españolas.   h un gran general importante. i un general grande e importante.   j un buen libro inglés.

Exercise 11 (Unit 19): a sinceramente **b** bien
c inteligentemente **d** puntualmente **e** mal **f** rápidamente
g seriamente **h** sinceramente **i** cuidadosamente **j** fácilmente

Exercise 12 (Unit 20): a de **b** que **c** de lo que **d** de
la que **e** que **f** de los que **g** de las que **h** del que
i que **j** de

Exercise 13 (Unit 22): *Suggested answers.* **a** Es sabrosísimo.
b Es rapidísimo. **c** Es comodísima. **d** Es elegantísimo.
e Es buenísima. **f** Son riquísimas. **g** Son dulcísimos.
h Son facilísimos. **i** Son guapísimas. **j** Son vivísimas.

Exercise 14 (Unit 25): a … pero el mío es más rápido.
b … pero la mía es más inteligente. **c** … pero los míos son
más trabajadores. **d** … pero las mías son más estúpidas.
e … pero el mío es más difícil. **f** … pero la mía es más
bonita. **g** … pero la mía es más hermosa. **h** … pero las
mías son más elegantes. **i** … pero el mío es más famoso.
j … pero las mías son más ricas.

Exercise 15 (Unit 27): a ti **b** él **c** usted **d** ustedes
e nosotros **f** vosotros **g** vosotras **h** nosotras

Exercise 16 (Unit 28): a No la he bebido, voy a beberla.
b No la he limpiado, voy a limpiarla. **c** No me he
duchado, voy a ducharme. **d** No lo he conducido, voy a
conducirlo. **e** No los he visto, voy a verlos. **f** No las he
lavado, voy a lavarlas.

Exercise 17 (Unit 32): a Nada. b Nunca. c En absoluto.
d Ya no. e Ningunos. f Nadie. g Nada. h En la vida.
i Todavía/Aún no. j Tampoco.

Exercise 18 (Unit 33): a del cual b la cual c la cual
d los cuales e el cual f las cuales

Exercise 19 (Unit 38): a hablamos b comemos c vivimos
d comes e vive f comen g habla h como i vivís
j hablan

Exercise 20 (Unit 39): a salgo; salimos b pongo; ponemos
c hago; hacemos d traigo; traemos e caigo; caemos
f doy; damos g voy; vamos h sé; sabemos i conduzco;
conducimos j conozco; conocemos

Exercise 21 (Unit 41): a eres b es c son d soy e es
f sois g es h son i es j es

Exercise 22 (Unit 41): a están b está c están d están
e está f estamos g Está; está h estáis i estoy j están

Exercise 23 (Unit 44): a dicen b friegas c pierdo
d vuelvo, vuelves; vuelve; vuelven e ríes; ríe; ríen

Exercise 24 (Unit 49): a duele b hace falta c hacen
falta; quedan d chifla e encanta f importa g toca
h falta i conviene j sienta

Exercise 25 (Unit 51): a acosté b dormí c oí
d desperté e senté f escuché g grité h contestó

i sentí j volví k empecé l llamó m salté n corrí
o abrí p descubrí q repetí r movió s acercó
t reconocí u vi v cerré w decidí

Exercise 26 (Unit 53): a quiso b dijo c produjo d hizo
e puso f repuso g dijeron h dije i puse j dijo
k supo l hicieron m pudo n condujeron o vinieron
p tuvieron q pusieron.

Exercise 27 (Unit 54): a éramos b vivíamos c vivían
d era e trabajaba f volvía g comíamos h jugábamos
i iba j entraba k estaba l bebía m veía n dormía
o pasábamos p acostábamos q esperábamos

Exercise 28 (Unit 55): a hacía b decidimos c hacía
d pusimos e quería f persuadió g venía h cogimos
i llovía j salimos k Eran l llegamos m entramos
n Era o estaba p oyó q Fue r empezó s tuvimos
t llegamos u estábamos v estaba w movía x podía

Exercise 29 (Unit 56): a Pagaré la cuenta mañana.
b Contestará a la carta mañana. c Repararán el coche
mañana. d Veremos la película mañana. e Volverás a
casa mañana. f Escribirá la carta mañana. g Irá a la
ciudad mañana. h Dormiremos aquí mañana. i Me
levantaré temprano mañana. j Os bañaréis en el mar
mañana.

Exercise 30 (Unit 63): a Se come la paella/La paella se come por toda España. **b** Se habla inglés en muchos países. **c** Se fuman muchos cigarrillos en la calle. **d** El vino tinto se bebe con frecuencia. **e** Las cartas se escriben con lápiz. **f** Se abre la puerta lentamente. **g** Se lee mucho este periódico. **h** Se come la hierba en el verano. **i** Se cogen las flores en el campo. **j** Se conoce el pueblo.

Exercise 31 (Unit 64): a Julio prefiere que nosotros descansemos. **b** Julio espera que Luisa gane la lotería. **c** Julio quiere que usted coma. **d** Julio necesita que Juan y María contesten. **e** Julio no quiere que (tú) fumes. **f** Julio quiere que los niños se laven. **g** Julio necesita que vosotros trabajéis. **h** Julio no quiere que la gente grite. **i** Julio no quiere que yo escriba. **j** Julio insiste en que las chicas beban.

Exercise 32 (Unit 65): a caiga **b** vea **c** tengamos **d** haga **e** pidas **f** diga **g** salgan **h** venga

Exercise 33 (Unit 68): a Si tuviese/tuviera dinero... **b** Si viviese/viviera en el campo... **c** Si supiese/supiera conducir... **d** Si viese/viera bien... **e** Si visitase/visitara a mis amigos... **f** Si bebiese/bebiera menos...

Exercise 34 (Unit 70): a Ojalá tuviese/tuviera dinero.
b Ojalá Julio me visitases/visitara. **c** Ojalá Elena me
escribiese/escribiera. **d** Ojalá mis padres fuesen/fueran
ricos. **e** Ojalá hablases/hablaras español.

Exercise 35 (Unit 71): a Abran el paquete. **b** Llenen el
depósito con agua. **c** No aparquen. **d** Paguen la cuenta
al salir. **e** No pisen la hierba. **f** No canten en el bar.

Exercise 36 (Unit 73): a hablaras **b** comieses **c** fuese
d fuéramos **e** saliese **f** bebieran **g** hablaseis
h dijera **i** hicieras **j** bebieses

Exercise 37 (Unit 78): a Había muchos burros en la playa.
b Ha habido un accidente. **c** Va a haber una corrida.
d Habrá muchos candidatos para el trabajo. **e** Sin dinero
habría una huelga. **f** Había habido un coche en el garaje.
g De repente hubo una llamada en la puerta. **h** No hay
servicios en el bar.

Exercise 38 (Unit 80): a podemos
b conoces **c** conoce **d** sabéis
e conoce **f** conoce **g** puedes
h sé **i** saben **j** sabéis

S	P	O	C	O	S	A
C	O	N	O	C	E	S
O	D	E	N	O	D	A
N	E	B	O	N	E	B
O	M	A	C	O	U	E
C	O	S	E	C	P	I
E	S	A	B	E	I	S

Exercise 39 (Unit 86): a ponerse **b** meter **c** colocar **d** aguantar **e** poner **f** meter **g** colocar **h** apagar **i** poner **j** ponerse.

Exercise 40 (Unit 88): a cojo **b** tomé **c** llevar **d** sacamos **e** sacamos **f** tomamos **g** sacamos **h** cogimos **i** cogimos **j** tardamos **k** saqué **l** tomé

Exercise 41 (Unit 94): a en **b** al **c** en **d** de **e** en **f** en **g** de **h** a **i** de **j** en **k** en **l** de **m** a **n** a **o** en **p** del **q** a **r** de **s** a

Exercise 42 (Unit 97): a hasta **b** desde **c** desde **d** hacia/para con **e** hacia **f** menos/salvo/excepto **g** durante **h** Según **i** sobre **j** durante

teach
yourself

spanish
juan kattán-ibarra

- Do you want to cover the basics then progress fast?
- Have you got rusty Spanish which needs brushing up?
- Do you want to reach a high standard?

Spanish starts with the basics but moves at a lively pace to give you a good level of understanding, speaking and writing. You will have lots of opportunity to practise the kind of language you will need to be able to communicate with confidence and understand the culture of speakers of Spanish.

spanish verbs
maría rosario hollis

- Do you want a handy reference guide to check verb forms?
- Are you finding tenses difficult?
- Do you want to see verbs used in a variety of contexts?

Spanish Verbs is a quick-and-easy way to check the form and meaning of over 3000 verbs. The clear layout makes the book very easy to navigate and the examples make the uses clear at the same time as building your vocabulary.